AVIS Viswanathan

Fall
like a
r🌹se
PETAL

*A father's lessons on how to be
happy and content while living
without money*

w

westland ltd
61, 2nd Floor, Silverline Building, Alapakkam Main Road, Maduravoyal, Chennai 600 09
No. 38/10 (New No.5), Raghava Nagar, New Timber Yard Layout, Bengaluru 560 026
93, 1st Floor, Sham Lal Road, Daryaganj, New Delhi 110 002

First published by westland ltd, 2014

10 9 8 7 6 5 4 3 2 1

ISBN: 978-93-84030-44-5

Cover design by Sowmya Nagarajan

Typeset: PrePSol Enterprises Pvt. Ltd.

A Sufi Master used to say to his disciples:

"A rose petal, so delicate, but so strong, doesn't hesitate about where it is falling, where it is going, whether there is any earth to find, to rest, to go to sleep, to die... Simply trust. Do not the petals flutter down just like that?"

Contents

Soul-speak On

'Fall Like A Rose Petal'

"Engaging primer on self-awareness and growth"

"I am struck by the raw honesty of AVIS's story. He opens out his heart and soul and shares a poignant journey. It could be the story of any one of us but I am not sure we would have the courage and compassion to bring it to Life. It takes a big heart and a kind acceptance to share one's story of trials, tribulations and triumph with openness and warmth.

The essence of finding one's peace in a zone of acute discomfort and dissonance is something many of us struggle with. It is with the spirit of generosity of the Universe and its people that we move forward. AVIS's narrative takes us on a ride, where he makes it easier for all of us to revisit our moments of deep discomfort and personal growth. *'Fall Like A Rose Petal'* is like a fellow partner in one's pursuit of reflection and personal clarity. The book lingers with thoughts of the grandness of Life's Vision and the minuteness of its course.

Whether you are a parent, struggling with the duality of parenthood, an entrepreneur on a roller coaster ride or a young professional on a personal quest, you will find something in this book which speaks to your soul. You will find yourself nodding in amazement, prodding with curiosity or simply feeling all wondrous about the duality of your concerns: growth in discomfort, strength in vulnerability, love in a pool of hatred and being okay even when not okay.

It is a beautiful story and great read but more so, it is an engaging primer on self-awareness and growth. You are bound to have deep thoughts on what matters once you have read *'Fall Like A Rose Petal'*."

Sairee Chahal, Founder,
www.sheroes.in, *New Delhi*

"Their story is a gift to the world"

"I admire this rare and candid confession that overcomes the stigma surrounding personal bankruptcy in the interest of sharing the experience to benefit others. Few would admit these failings. The shock, depression, social rejection, insult, threats and harassment that follow are real but the power and message of the book is the choice that AVIS and Vaani make to look at their predicament in the eye, admit their business failures and redefine themselves spiritually to face the consequences. All this, without compromising their core beliefs, self-esteem and integrity towards their children and creditors alike. Even with no immediate end in sight they persist. Heart-wrenching as it is, their story is a gift to the world to warn and prepare us for a very real possibility in these uncertain economic times."

Mansoor Khan, Film-maker, Organic Farmer, Author of 'The Third Curve', Coonoor

"FAITH forms the crux of AVIS's story"

"AVIS addresses his two children, speaking from his heart, stringing together a series of his financial misadventures, laced with betrayals of his trust. The turmoil is further compounded by the breach in relationship with his own family. AVIS's transparency is amazing, and through the spiritual voyage, he reveals his erroneous judgements, candid in each of his revelations.

There is not a trace of self-pity in the book, but an infinite belief in the Universe which gives as much as it receives. Right in the middle of financial crunches and not knowing where the next meal is coming from, AVIS and his very supportive wife Vaani are generous, forgiving and exude positive energy, which accounts for their surfacing each time they touch angst-ridden, rock-bottom situations. A string of miracles, knitted by the fabric of faith, opens many doors for the couple.

Always visualizing positive outcomes, AVIS has created magic in his own Life, through a voyage of self-discovery. Attributing all happenings to the cosmic design, AVIS and Vaani submit to the inevitable and in all humility ask for forgiveness for their shortcomings.

FAITH forms the crux of AVIS's story. This book is an inspiration to all those who are experiencing end-of-the-road situations. And where many look to suicide as the only way out, people like the Viswanathans show the way for survival through forgiveness, love and courage. A must-read for young executives, and for men and women in business too."

Sabita Radhakrishna,
Writer and Blogger, Chennai

"Simply a recipe on how to be more positive in Life"

"Back in 1996 when I founded Pizza Corner in India, AVIS and Vaani played a very active role in motivating and inspiring my team to become a world-class chain of Quick Service Restaurants across India and the region. On a personal level, AVIS never ceased to inspire me to become a better, more positive human being. *'Fall Like a Rose Petal'* is simply a recipe of how to become more positive in Life and how to convert a challenge into a positive opportunity. The book explains how, when you hope for the better, the better does happen to you. My favorite part in the book is the Afterword; AVIS goes on to list the simple principles that helped him and Vaani sustain happiness through very tough and agonizing times. The learnings from this book are great and extremely inspiring. I love a simple, yet powerful, statement on page 267: "Postpone everything else, but don't ever postpone being happy." To be happy - isn't that the very reason why we are all here on this planet?"

Antoine Bakhache, MD,
Bakhache Luxuries, Kuala Lumpur

About The Author

AVIS Viswanathan (47) is a happiness curator, Life Coach, inspired speaker, author and organizational transformation consultant who leads change management, culture and leadership development mandates in the corporate sector globally. He is currently a Principal Consultant at **a v initiatives**, a Specialist Consulting Firm that inspires Workplace Happiness.

AVIS is an acclaimed speaker whose Talks invoke soul, provoke thought and inspire action in the audiences he addresses. In the past, AVIS has been ranked among the top ten motivational speakers in India by *The Week* magazine.

AVIS confesses he did not make it to B-school. In fact, he barely scraped through college; thanks only, he says, to save his parents embarrassment. The first 10 years of his professional career were in the media, working with *The Indian*

Photo Credit: Bhargavii Mani

Aanchal, Aashirwad, Vaani and AVIS

Express, India Today, Businessworld and *Business Today*. He then briefly 'touched and felt' Life in the corporate sector in India, with global assignments. Those were highly eventful years, considering he was the globe-trotting EA (Executive Assistant) to Sterling Group's Chairman – maverick entrepreneur, C. Sivasankaran.

AVIS says he always lives inspired by Life! He sums up intelligent living: ***'Have Integrity Of Purpose, All Else Will Follow.'***

Note: AVIS' full name is Anand Viswanathan

Foreword

We have all been there. Not as devastatingly as Vaani and AVIS, perhaps, but who in the world is ever a stranger to adversity? Chances are that, at one time or another, we have felt the world collapse around us, or have stared at a seemingly insurmountable wall, or have asked oneself the question: *"Why me?"*. I certainly don't want one to lose sight of the deep-rooted socio-political-economic problems that often lie at the core. But that's of precious little help on your personal front – which is always here and now! What do you do when crisis stares you in the face? What do you do when it refuses to go away? Vaani and AVIS have an answer for us – ***'Fall Like A Rose Petal'***!

This book documents an incredible journey by a courageous couple through their insanely difficult times of financial misery. The cascade of anecdotes itself makes an engaging read. But what makes the book special is the simple yet profound insight it offers: the only way to prevent a crisis from overwhelming you is by living Life to the fullest – with joy, dignity and Purpose. Societal norms encourage you to cower down, be apologetic and live a glum, sub-human existence in your troubled times. That's what's supposed to be natural. But Vaani and AVIS did the unnatural – and they invite us to do the same. Time and again, when they seemed to have reached the end of the road, they found a way to turn it around. And most importantly, through this gnawing uncertainty and misery, they found a way to carry on living lives befitting that of a human being – unapologetic, poised, spirited, self-respecting and happy.

I met AVIS and Vaani for the first time just about a year and a half ago in Chennai. My movie *'Chittagong'* was playing at the Chennai International Film Festival. It was an evening reception and I practically knew nobody there. I was getting ready to duck out, when I ran into AVIS. To my surprise, he knew about me and my movie – and the battles I endured in making the movie. I was touched and reassured by AVIS' enthusiasm. Reading the book today and looking back, I now realize what they must have been going through. But I didn't get even an inkling of their troubles then. What I remember of that December evening in Chennai is a man who was passionate and who had the most positive outlook to Life! I guess that's what **'Fall Like A Rose Petal'** is all about – maintaining your inner balance even when things around you come unglued.

My foray into movie-making was not an easy one. I was going through Life just fine – a senior research scientist with NASA (The National Aeronautics and Space Administration agency of the United States of America) with a number of inventions and awards, a settled and happy family

Life. But, somewhere down the line I realized I was not utilizing my potential to the fullest. So, one fine morning, I gave it all up. I quit NASA and staked everything to follow my passion – film-making. Slowly and painstakingly, *'Chittagong'* was born. But in the process – my Life spun out of control, including the loss of my son, Ishan, to a bizarre accident. Ishan was incredibly close to me.

Completely alone and practically penniless, it felt like Life had lost all meaning. It was in one of those moments, Shankar-Ehsan-Loy (what amazingly humble and talented people these three are!) – who did the music for my movie – came up with the song *"Bolo Na"*, penned by the supremely talented Prasoon Joshi. The song fetched the National Award to both Shankar Mahadevan and Prasoon Joshi. But the larger point here is that creation always carries its own resonance. Strange as it seems, the song became an anchor for me in those dark and horrific days. Slowly the world began swinging back into perspective. I realized that I was really not alone. I realized that there's much more to Life than wallowing in one's misfortunes. Things began to fall in place ... but that's another story for another time.

As I read **'Fall Like A Rose Petal'**, I relived all my battles within, of the last four years. I guess I had learnt that if there's something you need to do – go ahead and do it. It may not work out the way you imagined, but Life finds a way. That's just the way it is. Creativity has probably found a solution long before your logical mind has invented it. Logic and habit are products of the existing rules and are constrained by them, but creation and new beginnings happen by flouting existing rules and prejudices. Whatever it is, there is simply no reason to allow your woes to dominate and emasculate your existence. AVIS and Vaani's story only served to reinforce a belief I have come to hold sacred in the last few years. Faced with problems, you do not swerve from fulfilling your mission. You make your plans and strategies, you march ahead with full commitment and passion – and you don't worry what the outcome would be. That is probably what is called living in the moment. It is not being reckless or fickle. It is having faith in the strength of your plans and the endless possibilities and opportunities that the world always offers. There's simply no telling which doors will open where.

'Fall Like A Rose Petal' is not an operations manual telling you exactly what to do when you are faced with a crisis. Nor does it give you readymade solutions that you apply like a magic wand. If you are looking for something like that – you would be disappointed. They don't exist. But what AVIS and Vaani's journey does tell you is that a solution exists – it can be found! Their journey will make you think, will make you question, make you look inward, and help you realize that it **can be done**. And above all, it will make you believe in this great and ongoing project called 'humanity'. Charlie

Chaplin, the great film-maker, had once said, "Nothing is permanent in this world, not even our damned troubles." So what are you waiting for? Be ready to reinvent and re-engage.

But, of course, before all of that, read the book.

Bedabrata Pain
June 2014

Bedabrata Pain is a film-maker, a former NASA-scientist and an inventor of digital camera technologies. He lives mostly in Los Angeles and Mumbai.

To our 179 Angels,
who helped us survive, find meaning in
Life and
awaken to a beautiful way of living!

Introduction

"We are not human beings going through a temporary spiritual experience; we are spiritual beings going through a temporary human experience."

~ Anonymous

Dear Reader,

In the wee hours of Tuesday, January 1, 2008, just past 1 AM, while the world was still ringing in the New Year, my soul-mate, friend, wife and business partner, Vaani and I sat on the ground in our bedroom in Bishop Garden,[1] Chennai. I was finishing my last peg of whisky, thanks to a caring friend who had brought the drink and dinner over.

We had no money that night; we could not even afford a bottle of Royal Challenge whisky, a favourite Indian domestic brand, which then cost about ₹500 or $10![2] We reviewed our Life. I don't

---

[1] Bishop Garden – an upmarket residential neighbourhood in south Chennai.

[2] ₹50.00 = US (United States) $ 1.00 all through this book; which was the exchange value around the time much of this story happened.

xxiv   AVIS Viswanathan

know if the night outside was darker or our lives together seemed to be. We had *no* money; definitely no money in the bank, at best we had ₹2000 (less than $40[3]) between our wallets that night; we had no assets and we had no friends who would help us anymore. We had borrowed from several of them already. We had borrowed from the whole world, it appeared. We had two kids to take care of. Our son Aashirwad, (Aash, then 18), who had just got admission to the University of Chicago (ranked among the world's best schools for Economics) and our daughter Aanchal, (Aanch, then 13), who was in high school. Life for us, at 40, it seemed, was over.

That night, maybe on a high on account of the alcohol, or maybe on a low because of the circumstances – I cried. And then I hugged Vaani and whispered in her ear, "We don't have a choice. We have to claw our way back. And win, *Mom*. Thanks for being there for me and for us."

She hugged me tight, kissed me and said, "*Dad*, I am there with you, however long this takes. We have to win."

The experience that Vaani and I are still going through has changed our lives. We had a small

---

[3] ₹2000 - This is exactly the money that AVIS and Vaani had left with them that night; no assets, no investments, no stock options to fall back on, no insurance, no health insurance and no gold jewellery too that could be hawked to raise cash.

Firm, **image*equity*+®**, that was set up in August 1996, with the Vision of becoming *the* Indian Consulting Firm for the world from India. We practiced Reputation Management, a novel concept in building organizational culture (internal) and respect (external) – as both aspects contribute to an organization's reputation. A few strategic mistakes and the poor execution of our Vision led our Firm to bankruptcy and burdened us with over a million dollars in debt. Most of our debt was taken in our personal capacities, from banks, family, friends and private lenders – both the *Marwari*[4] type and the ferocious 10%-per-month-interest-rate usurers, called 'speed money' or '*kanthu vatti*[5] lenders in Tamil Nadu.

Life was so scary at that moment: *How do you survive with ₹2000, with a family to look after; with kids to educate? More importantly, how do you deal with 179 creditors of all shapes and sizes? How can you even fathom repaying a million dollars when you don't have any income and zero prospects of business improving? Why were we going through all this? Was there a way out? Would we live to tell our tale?*

As you can see, we have survived; we have lived through, and continue to live through, some very

---

[4]   *Marwari* – a community of businessmen in India, some of whom are money lenders.

[5]   *Kanthu vatti* – an usurious practice of lending money for 10% interest per month.

challenging years. Our experience is certainly not complete. Not yet. Whose is, anyway? We continue to learn. We still have our million dollar debt to repay. Though we have reinvented ourselves and now have a Firm, '**a v initiatives**', to better represent our transformed business model, our business has yet to pick up. Our Vision for our Firm, though undiluted, is yet to be realized. Our problems remain. The upside is that our ability to deal with each of our problems has gone up phenomenally! More significantly, our awakening is complete. We are no longer scared of *Life*; or insecure. Faith has replaced fear and we have developed boundless patience.

This book explores the nature and continuum of Life. There is no beginning to our story. There is no end either. There are simply experiences, such as this one. I hope this book changes your Life. Just as the experiences captured in these pages changed mine!

This book was not just born out of the fact that I can write or the need to express myself. It captures learnings from this Life-changing experience. Of hopelessness. Of insolvency. Of bankruptcy. Of penury. And also of faith, patience, love, companionship, abundance and *soul*. Of integrity and of leading a principled Life, despite temptations to take the 'easy way' out of painful or messy situations. Our experience has taught us what the phrase 'the milk of human kindness' really means. We have seen and continue to witness miracles happen, often with strangers walking into our lives to rescue us, each time we were convinced it was all over. I have written this book in the hope that you can benefit from what I am sharing and discover the right way of thinking, living, working and winning in Life – for yourself.

These pages capture several actual experiences that Vaani and I have been through. We share our learnings frankly because we believe we can inspire others who are struggling with Life. Even so, let me clarify. This is not *Guru*-speak. This is not a religious tome. This is not about a God and His miracles. This is about an ordinary, educated couple; middle-class, upwardly mobile professionals – who lost everything material in Life. Not in some bygone era, but in the very first decade of this millennium, and who still cling to hope and to each other. Who have faith in their companionship, in their business and in a Higher Energy.

You will not find methods to live 'intelligently' here. There are no models presented here either. This book may not even always appeal to the intellect. It is from the soul, for the soul. This is pure soul-speak.

As the experiences I share here are unique and deeply personal, it may well be possible that you may differ with us, on some occasions, on the choices we made and the decisions we took. And I believe that's fine. Because even if you disagree with what we did, you may still be able to relate to the lessons we have learnt through the choices we made.

The book's title and treatment are inspired by Osho, the Master[6], who, in *Just Like That*, says, while sharing an old Sufi story, so beautifully: *"A Sufi Master used to say to his disciples: "A rose petal, so delicate, but so strong, doesn't hesitate about where it is falling, where it is going, whether there is any earth to find, to rest, to go to sleep, to die... Simply trust. Do not the petals flutter down just like that?""*

This book, therefore, is an invitation to you, dear reader, to learn to trust Life and accept it for what it is, the way it is. Just as a rose petal does. Just like us, Vaani and me. All our suffering – yours and mine – arises from questioning what happens to us. Instead, if we trust Life's Master Plan and celebrate living our Life exactly the way it is unfolding, without resisting anything, we will be in bliss, irrespective of our circumstances.

Each chapter in this book began with the notes I wrote in my personal journal between January 2007 and October 2013, almost daily, to my two children, Aashirwad and Aanchal. Vaani and I had refrained from sharing the gory details of our financial situation with our children though we did not try too hard to conceal the information from them either. I wrote those notes to chronicle the

---

[6] Osho, the Master – an Indian spiritual thinker who transited this planet between 1931 and 1990.

experiences we were going through, so that our children could learn from them, whenever they read them, as they set out on their lives' journeys.

A few of them are being shared now to act as a beacon of hope for those who want to live in this world and yet be above it. These are true instances of trust, faith, love, pain, remorse, self-doubt, motivation, Purpose, parenting and personal courage. This book celebrates the inscrutability of Life and leads you to the path of following your bliss and finding joy from within. Since it was born out of a real-Life experience, I hope it will strike a chord with you.

Each chapter has a standalone anecdote(s) and has a learning drawn from the experience(s) shared in it. The title of each chapter summarizes the learning contained in it. The stories are recounted in no particular chronological order, though you will find dates, places and events mentioned to help you relate better to the experience. When you read Chapter 6, *'What Goes Around Comes Around'*, you will find that while the chapter is addressed to both my children, it also addresses you, the reader. That is so because Aashirwad did know what was going on to some extent, yet the relevant note in the journal was diligently written out because Aanchal had to be told this story at some point in time.

Names and identities have been changed upon request or protected, though none of the events

or dates is fictional. Some events have been
deliberately described in greater detail, while
others have been kept brief to limit the exposure
of the people involved in them. A few incidents,
however crucial they may have been to our lives,
have been omitted to protect our privacy or those
of the people connected with them or both. We
seek your understanding on this.

For this book, I have selected only a few of the
over 2000 notes, I had written to my children over
these years. You can read the notes/chapters,
sequentially or at random. The chapters are
arranged to allow you to browse through the book
as you want. I have tried not to preach but have
merely shared my journey as an ordinary mortal,
trying to make sense of what Life is; enriched and
inspired, nevertheless, by the experience so far!

I am extremely grateful to Life for this experience.
I am not bitter. I, hopefully, am better from it.
Without it, there would be no book. Without the
book, I would not have had this opportunity to
connect with you and share.

Ours is a story of bankruptcy. Yours may have
a different angle to it. Life happens to each of us
differently. But the learnings we need to gather
from Life are common. So, while I am not sure
everything in this book will directly apply to your
Life, I believe it will definitely appeal to you. Just
knowing that you are not alone, irrespective of
what you are going through, whatever it may be,

can be comforting and help you hold on and hope for one more day. And then another. And then one more. You live Life, one day at a time, one moment at a time, making each one count. This is what Vaani and I did and continue to do. This is the most valuable lesson we have learnt from this excruciatingly painful time.

Hope you can relate to it. Hope it inspires you. Hope it changes your Life!

With Prayers,
AVIS Viswanathan
Chennai
November 2013

1

Of Living In The Moment

"Take sips of this pure wine being poured. Don't mind that you've been given a dirty cup."

~ Mevlana Jalaluddin Rumi,
13th Century Persian Poet

Monday, March 17, 2008
8.40 PM: On board 9W 487[7] to Chennai

Dear Aash and Aanch,

This morning, we had just ₹1000 ($20). This was all the money we had left as a family. No assets, no savings in the bank, nothing. Just ₹1000. We are bankrupt as a Firm and insolvent as a family. Survival seems impossible. Yet, *Mom* gave me ₹500 of the cash left with us as I pulled on my jacket to leave for Mumbai at 4 AM to meet a potential client.

The client is a well-meaning and professional CEO (Chief Executive Officer). He had arranged for my tickets, though he need not have. As I boarded the flight to Mumbai and fastened my seat belt, I was informed by the flight attendant that I had been upgraded to Business Class, being the frequent-flier that I am, or was, until business slowed down! The irony hit me hard as we got airborne. 50% of our net worth as a family was sitting in my wallet. There was just another ₹500 at home. And I was sure *Mom* would have been as nervous as I was about the fate of the client meeting. The only reason I clung to hope was, as I asked myself – why would a client fly me out, at his cost, if he was

---

[7] 9W 487 – an evening service flight operated by India's Jet Airways between Mumbai and Chennai.

not serious about the engagement? Yet even as my mind veered towards worry, I tried to hold it still to attend to the beautiful morning sky. The world always looks so much more pristine from 30,000 feet above! In some time, I had become peaceful and felt that I had dissolved into the Universe.

It was in that calm and peaceful frame of mind that I arrived in Mumbai. The client's office had arranged for a peak-cap wearing chauffeur with a Toyota Camry (a luxury car from the Toyota stable), to come to the airport to pick me up and drive me to their office at Nariman Point, on the 20th floor of Express Towers. Kishore Kumar's immortal – and most apt at that moment – ode to Life, *'Zindagi ka safar, hai yeh kaisa safar'*[8] (*Safar*, 1970) played on the car's FM radio for some part of the ride downtown. The irony could not have been starker. I was torn between the peace that I valued so much and the anxiety that refused to leave me alone. I wish I had my mind on money, but in reality, I had money on my mind!

When I reached Express Towers and our client greeted me in his office, I was overwhelmed when he sat me down and offered me some coffee. It was a normal act of courtesy but this morning it meant hope and warmth, in an extremely cold, deprived,

---

[8] *'Zindagi ka safar, hai yeh kaisa safar'* – meaning 'This journey of Life, what kind of a journey is it?' is a song celebrating the inscrutability of Life written by Indeevar and set to music by Kalyanji Anandji

and fearful (about our future as a Firm and as a family) scenario. Our client excused himself after the coffee and pleasantries, saying he needed to finish a meeting ahead of ours. I was left alone in the meeting room for some time.

I was tense and I stood up to watch the beautiful Marine Drive, on this bright March morning, which was abuzz below me. As I watched the traffic move, sometimes swiftly, sometimes at a crawl, I caught myself crying. I believe I cried involuntarily, because the moment, its cruel irony and its unbeatable beauty, was so very overwhelming. Here I was, not even worth ₹1000 in the difficult-to-escape materialistic sense, with a family and Firm which were dependent on me; in reality, presiding over the ruins of a bankrupt, debt-laden business, yet, symbolically, at that moment, I was presiding over some of the most expensive real estate in the world, having flown Business Class to Mumbai, driven downtown in a Toyota Camry, and waiting to sign a contract that would mean both resuscitation and resurrection!

Our client came back in some time with our engagement letter and an advance cheque. Of course, I knew that signing that contract would in no way solve or end our problems. But I also instantly realized that this was a sign from the Universe that we were being looked after!

As I took the cheque with trembling hands and signed the engagement documents, I remember wondering, intensely, curiously, is this *Life*? Where you can, and have to, see, live and accept *only* what you have in a given moment? As it turns out, and as I have learnt from and in Life over the years, this is indeed *Life*! It is what it is! The best way to live Life is to live in the moment, the only one that you can call your own!

As long as you take Life one day at a time, one event at a time, one moment at a time, while having your long-term Vision etched firmly in your mind, you will *never* have a problem with Life! *Living is all about being what you are, the way you are and accepting circumstances the way they are!* Whatever you are handed, make it count. Don't rue your fate or wish things could be different. Just visualize what you want the future to be like, and while keeping that Vision intact, live in the present, making the best of the situation you find yourself in!

Love You Both Every Moment,
Dad

2

Never Ever Give Up!

"Our greatest glory is not in never falling, but in rising every time we fall."

~ Confucius, Chinese Philosopher
and Teacher (551 BC ~ 479 BC)

Tuesday, April 17, 2007
9.30 PM: Chennai

Dear Aash and Aanch,

Today, our first cheque bounced at the bank.

Over the last two years, my single-minded focus had been to ensure that no cheque bounced. Indeed, over time, we had begun borrowing from Peter to pay Paul. But when the first cheque bounced today, I was distraught. I felt defeated. I tried to anchor within. Standing amidst the noisy traffic on Haddows Road, outside the bank in the early Chennai summer heat, I anchored in *mouna* – a method of practising silence that I had picked up in 2005. *Mouna* works brilliantly and I practice it diligently every day.

Even as I anchored within, my gut was telling me that it was all over. I knew that a single cheque bouncing was something we could explain away and live with. However, as the Operations Head of our business, I knew this was an early warning sign of a bigger problem – of a dark period of acute cashlessness coming our way. We were never going to be able to borrow any more money from the market with a pockmarked bank statement, detailing instances of cheque bounces.

Just as I had begun to feel secure in the spell of *mouna,* a car pulled out of the parking slot in front of me, and almost magically, another one, a deep purple Maruti Zen (a popular Indian car model at the time) pulled in. As the driver adjusted his vehicle in the slot and stepped out, a little sticker on the car's rear windscreen grabbed my attention. It read: '*Never Ever Give Up!*'.

Call it a strange coincidence or call it cosmic design; to me, to us, those four words were magical and meant everything at that moment!

Sometimes, you just want to give up. Giving up, you will want to believe, is an option. Running away, you will convince yourself, is a solution. Nothing could really be further from the truth. Is throwing in the towel an option for those that do not even possess a towel? Sometimes, Life does put you in the dock. Your business faces tough times. Maybe your relationship becomes strained. Or your work-Life balance becomes unbalanced; you have no time for yourself. In such times, external reference points are not worth examining or leaning upon for support.

The only place to find peace and solace in, is to go within. The practice of silent periods, *mouna* – when you, and not the environment around you, falls silent – is the only, I repeat, **only**, route available to escape the tyranny of (such a) time! *Mouna* will not change your external reality. Neither will it make your problems go away. However, it will definitely help you deal with your problems in a better manner. Do you worry about your heart if your shirt is stained or torn? It is the exterior which is disturbed or distressed. Not what lies within. Similarly, a challenged business or a strained relationship does not imply that **you** are a failure or that **you** are bad! It simply means the fabric of your external environment is under pressure. You are still pure and despite the circumstances, unstained. *Mouna* will help you see this reality and experience it.

Coming back to the towel analogy, whose towel are you throwing? Did Life send you into this world with a towel? Or did you acquire the towel, which you threw in, during this lifetime? The towel is representative of what you are not. Your true nature does not include a towel – a job, a degree, a social status, a companion, a house, a car, a bank balance – and therefore, if you must concede something or if you do give up something, know also that it has nothing to do with the real **you**!

This is downright simple. You are not all the 'things' that you think you are. You are above all of this and you must learn to see every situation, every trial and every tribulation as an experience. If you allow yourself to be affected by external realities, you will feel depressed and beaten. Live in the eye of the storm. Be peaceful at the core. Remain untouched.

The truth is we are all one with the Universe. Whenever you experience that oneness, even if it is for a brief while, particularly through a period of silence, through *mouna* or otherwise, when your energy and the Universe's energy are aligned on the same frequency, the Universe will send you a sign. That is what happened to me this morning. The Universe, through that sticker on the rear windscreen of the car, told me, and us, never to give up! And I believe and I know that we will come out of this phase of Life, enriched and enlightened!

Let's Keep Walking,
Dad

3

Let Go And Ye Shall Receive

"Life has no back doors. You cannot steal Life. You cannot be a thief. Life gives, and gives infinitely and gives unconditionally. You please be just in a let-go."

~ Osho, the Master (transited through Planet Earth between 1931 and 1990)

Thursday, June 4, 2009
9 PM: Chennai

Dear Aash and Aanch,

L ast Sunday, May 31, 2009, our two cars, a Hyundai Accent and a Hyundai Santro (popular models from Hyundai at that time), were seized by the bank from our home. It was the outcome of a mediated arrangement I had arrived at with the bank. I had been unable to pay the EMIs (equated monthly instalments) on our car loans regularly for over 18 months.

The bankers had told me that they would be forced to seize the vehicles if our outstanding amount went past six EMIs per vehicle. The manager in charge of my defaulting accounts was a wonderful human being called Krishnan Subramaniam.[9] He was moved by our story. He believed totally in *Mom* and me and had told me that even though he was under intense pressure from his seniors, he would not seize the vehicles without prior and sufficient notice to me. However, on May 1st he sent me a text message saying he was moving to a new job at another bank. He told me that a colleague of his at my bank would be in touch and that a seizure seemed imminent and unavoidable at this time. Our loan accounts were

---

[9]   Real name not disclosed to protect identity.

showing seven months of default and an eighth month had begun in May.

Mom and I were initially very depressed and unable to reconcile ourselves to this 'loss'. Yes, we had lost money, but now, we would lose our source of mobility, as well as our reputation! In India, from the neighbours to the maid, everyone would whisper about the cars being seized and people would look at you differently. Besides, what would we tell you, if you called from Chicago, Aash? You would then have to bear the burden of this unnecessary worry as you write your finals this week to complete your second year in college. Even if we didn't tell you over the phone, you would know of it when you came home in another fortnight for your summer break. And Aanch would not be able to comprehend why things like these were happening.

Finally, we realized we couldn't delay this anymore. *Mom* and I decided, on Friday, May 29th, to just let go. I spoke to the bank and arranged for them to come at 3 PM on Sunday, May 31st and take away the vehicles. We knew most people in our apartment block would be enjoying their Sunday afternoon siesta, Aanch would be busy with something or the other in her room and your Venks[10] *thatha*[11] too would be asleep. The team from the bank came at the appointed hour and

---

[10] Venks – Venks Venkatachalam, Vaani's father.

[11] *'Thatha'* – means grandfather in Tamil.

the whole seizure process was completed in 15 minutes as all the documentation was in place. The cars were driven out of our parking lot even as *Mom* and I bade them a solemn goodbye. When things are taken away from you, you feel a sense of loss. *Mom* and I felt that sense of loss; it was as if a part of us had been snatched away.

Just the previous day, Saturday, May 30th, Uncle Shekar and Aunty Shanti had taken *Mom* and me out to lunch to Cascade Restaurant at Besant Nagar[12]. Uncle Shekar noticed our Accent car, clean and gleaming as always, and wondered how old the car was.

I replied, "Three years."

He said he marvelled at how well we had maintained it!

I smiled and replied, "Well, Shekar, today's the last day of the cars being with us. And we have cleaned and polished them as we normally do."

I have always believed in sharing with people, even if it made me vulnerable. Which is why you will find, I always wear my Life on my sleeve! Uncle Shekar was surprised when I told him about the impending seizure. He knew we had problems, but he confessed he did not know they were so serious.

He excused himself, conferred in whispers with Aunty Shanti and after a few minutes, looked up

---

[12] Besant Nagar – an upmarket residential neighbourhood in South Chennai

at me and *Mom* and said, "AVIS and Vaani, we have two cars as you know. And we don't need two. Take our smaller car, the Hyundai Getz (another popular model from Hyundai), and keep it as long as you want. You can return it to us whenever you are able to."

I was flabbergasted. *Mom* was in tears. It wasn't the availability of their spare car that overwhelmed us. *It was the timing of their offer and the reality sinking in that though we would have our two cars being taken away on Sunday, we would not be car-less!* To imagine that, just the previous day, Friday, we had decided to let go and reconciled ourselves to a Life without cars, at least for the immediate future! While thanking Uncle Shekar profusely, I told him we were touched and wanted him to be sure he wanted to part with his Getz for an indefinite – at that moment – period of time.

He, in turn, said, "Shut up AVIS! Just come and take it. It's yours!"

Mom and I had nothing more to say. The next morning after our cars were taken away, Monday, June 1st, we picked up Uncle Shekar's Getz and Aanch went to school in that car! She was a bit surprised when we told her we had sold our cars because we wanted to meet Aash's University fees and said we had borrowed Uncle Shekar's car for the time being. I am sorry we lied to you Aanch, but we felt, for the time being at least, you should be spared the details. When Aanch got into the

Getz, she was delighted it had a music system that played CDs. Our cars had only been capable of playing primitive audio cassettes! She forgot all about our cars and was lost in the world of music. At least she had nothing much other than school to worry about!

On Tuesday, June 2nd, a former client and now a close friend of ours, a serial entrepreneur and mentor to many IT companies, Rajesh Narasimhan,[13] called from Bengaluru. We spoke almost twice every month and he had been helping me, and *Mom*, deal with the bankruptcy. Aash, you will recall having breakfast with him at home at the end of August 2008, a few weeks before you left to join college in Chicago that September. Uncle Rajesh loved the *idlis*[14] and *sambar*[15] *Mom* had made that morning.

Uncle Rajesh was also the first person to point out to me that we were bankrupt. In those weeks and months in 2007, when I was desperately pinging every friend on SMS asking for cash, primarily to help manage the creditors, Uncle Rajesh had once thundered over the phone, "AVIS, for God's sake, **stop** paying your creditors for now. **You are bankrupt.** Do you get it? **Get this straight.** Your recovery is going to take years and a lot of faith and hard, solid work! First focus on the family,

---

[13] Real name not disclosed to protect identity.
[14] *'Idlis'* – steamed rice cakes, a South Indian breakfast .
[15] *'Sambar'* – a lentil-based broth, to go with the *idlis*.

then try to get the business on track and **only then** begin repayment to creditors."

So, on the phone call on June 2nd, Uncle Rajesh enquired about both of you and wanted an update. I told him the cars had been repossessed and how Uncle Shekar's car had miraculously arrived. And how grateful we were to the Universe and to people.

Uncle Rajesh, spontaneously, responded, "AVIS, I have an extra car that I wanted to give away. It's a sedan[16]. You can keep it. You don't even need to pay for it now. Pay when able. Just keep it. You can return your other friend's car. This one is yours. Just imagine you owe me nothing."

He went on, dismissing my feeble protests, that he need not go out of the way, to say that I could have it driven down from Bengaluru or he could arrange for it. I thanked him, hung up, discussed his call with *Mom*, and we decided to accept his offer.

So this evening, Prasad, our regular cabbie in Bengaluru, arrived, driving Uncle Rajesh's sedan, which is in top condition. Suddenly it struck me and *Mom* that despite both our own cars being taken away; here we were, in the same week, with two cars standing in our parking lot! *Mom* and I decided to return Uncle Shekar's car to him though because we did not want to take advantage of anyone's generosity.

---

[16] The gentleman who gave this car to us did not want us to mention its make/model

We had let go. The Universe, without our asking, gave us not one, but two cars, through its angelic, marvellous creations – Uncle Shekar, Aunty Shanti and Uncle Rajesh – all in the same week!

I must also tell you both that on Monday, May 25th, just 10 days ago; I did a workshop titled **'surfboarder'** for the top management of Manipal Hospitals in Bengaluru. At the end of the session, the CEO of the hospital, impressed with the impact I had made on his team, gave me, along with the cheque for my fee, a wooden toy car, a Rolls Royce model, made by the famous handicraft artisans of Channapatna, near Mysore. He said he was giving it to me because this was the only memento his team could source when he asked them to procure one at short notice. I remember calling *Mom* from the airport and telling her that their choice of memento was indeed 'weird'. A wooden, handcrafted, Rolls Royce *toy car*?

Now, when I look back and connect the sequence of events, it all makes sense. We are under pressure to let go of our cars. A toy car arrives but I am unable to read the symbolism in the Universe's indication that a car is on its way. We let go of our cars. The next day the Getz arrives. The same week the sedan arrives. *Aha!* Wasn't the Universe telling me and *Mom*, much more than all this, that *'all is and will be well'*? Perhaps, it really, really was!

This was a miracle. But not one that is difficult to comprehend. Let me explain. The learning here is simple: the more you hold on, cling to something, the more you suffer. And the less you witness Life's miracles. The Universe and Life, operate on a simple principle. The principle, as I have come to understand it, is 'nothingness'. Nothingness is what you and I are all about. You came with nothing. You will go with nothing. This earthly sojourn is where you will deceive yourself to believe that you gained a lot.

You imagine you gained an experience called a 'lifetime'; you gained an education, a name, fame, family, wealth or reputation. All this is what you **think** you gain. But will you be able to take any of these with you when you depart? Even this experience called a lifetime may not be remembered by you. Who knows? Because Life, after this body's demise, is unknown to you and me! So, why do we cling to anything, and everything; wasting precious time, energy and effort?

We have seen this time and again. And you both will do well to remember this in your lives, through this story of our cars – that the moment you let go, you receive.

For, how can we receive when our hands, our minds and our hearts, are full of things that we refuse to let go of?

Live Letting Go,
Dad

4

Understand, Never Interpret

"*The reality of the other person is not in what he reveals to you, but in what he cannot reveal to you. Therefore, if you would understand him, listen not to what he says but rather to what he does not say.*"

~ Khalil Gibran, Lebanese-American Artist, Poet, Writer (1883 ~ 1931)

Sunday, September 5, 2010
7 PM: Chennai

Dear Aash and Aanch,

C an someone whom you dismissed from employment ever teach you anything? Well, had it not been for Prateik,[17] I may never have learned that this was possible.

Today is Teacher's Day in India. And I learned a very powerful, humbling lesson in being human from a former member of my team whom I had fired, unceremoniously, for non-performance on the job.

Aash would remember the second team member of our Firm, recruited in 1997, when we operated out of our home in Veena Apartments, R. A. Puram[18], Chennai. His name is Prateik. The very first team member Jeyasekhar had just joined us as an office assistant. Prateik called me the very next day, asking for a job. I am not sure how he heard of us. Nevertheless, he met all the criteria that we were looking for in an Executive Assistant. He was young, just out of college, and was willing to work hard – come early and even work weekends if required. He had a sense of humour, which could at times end up becoming a liability

---

[17] Real name not disclosed to protect identity.
[18] R.A. Puram – a residential and commercial neighbourhood in South Chennai

in client meetings, but was still good fun. He fit my definition of someone who wasn't an MBA, but was a PSD – poor, smart, with a deep desire to be rich!

I used to be a workaholic at that time. And Prateik and Jeyasekhar would come to work by 7 AM most days and stay well past 9 PM. Since we were a start-up, working out of our home, they would eat with us at our own dining table and had become virtually a part of the family.

1997 was an important year for our Firm. We signed up three clients that year. And Prateik played an important role in the signing-up process. We celebrated each client win with a party, drinking together at different bars each time. For Prateik, all of this and the work we did was new, and he dedicated himself to handling our clients with passion and curiosity.

He had some issues though. He was not very organized, never made a checklist and often, both the client and I found him apologizing for not carrying documentation and folders to client meetings. Now, in our system, an Executive Assistant (EA) working alongside me was training to be an independent Client Owner and Prateik often fell short of my expectations in that regard.

One day he forgot to pack a critical resource, a recorded audio cassette (CDs and MP3s had not replaced the ubiquitous audio cassette back then) that contained a customized song,

for a workshop at Apollo Hospitals[19]. In leading
change management workshops on the shop-
floors of client establishments, I hated unwanted
surprises. Whether they were those delivered
by clients, like bad venue or poor quality
microphones, or those caused by my own team.
That morning the crisis was fuelled by Prateik
not packing that audio cassette from which I was
to play a song whose lyrics were to emphasize a
very important change that we wanted to see in
the client's team. I was livid, yet I carried on with
the workshop. It was a mediocre session in my
opinion and could have been far better had the
musical element been present!

I came back home, walked into my office, with
Prateik following me. I sat in my chair, looked
Prateik in the eye and told him: "You are fired!"

I didn't ask for an explanation, though he offered
one, while mumbling apologies. I forced him to
submit his resignation, even as Jeyasekhar looked
on, walked him to the front door and saw him
out. It was a cold and now when I reflect upon it,
perhaps unreasonable way to handle a crisis with
the first executive cadre recruit of our aspiring-to-
be-global Firm.

That night Prateik called me. In those days
mobile telephony had just come to India and the
world was still to wake up to the power of the

---

[19] Apollo Hospitals – India's leading healthcare chain and
    imag*equity*+®'s first client

Internet and email. So, Prateik's call to our home landline was not a very pleasant thing to happen. It was intrusive.

He said, in a shaky voice, "AVIS, you have thrown me out on the street. You have ruined my career. You have hit me below the belt."

I remember replying animatedly: "Son, you caused your own downfall by refusing to learn. Your sacking was your own doing. Learn from this episode, never repeat it. You are a capable young man and you will do very well if you learn what not to do in Life."

I put the phone down. He must have tried again, because the phone kept ringing several times afterward, but I did not pick it up.

Our Firm's first executive team member's journey with us was over.

It was in 2005 that Prateik walked into our office again. We had long moved out as a family from Veena Apartments and the whole apartment was now an office. I happened to step out into the front office and I found Prateik trying to convince the receptionist that he must be allowed to meet me though he did not have an appointment. We hugged each other and enquired about each other's families. I invited Prateik to come into my office and offered him some tea. Prateik shared how he had actually benefitted from the 'sacking' and thanked me profusely, for making a man out of him. He said he had found a job, after ours, in South Africa. He had practised a new work ethic and grown fast to become the company's country manager. He said he had carried the lessons from whatever he had learned in the months that he worked for me, with us, in his heart, all these years.

"You, AVIS, have guided me in more ways than you will even know!" he declared, profusely embarrassing me.

I also learned from him that his sister had died, a victim of dowry harassment. I gave him strength, asked him to practice *mouna*, and told him to learn to accept Life for what it is. He candidly observed that he was surprised to see a 'calmer, more evolved AVIS'. We shook hands, hugged each other and he left promising to be in touch.

The next time I heard from him was at the end of 2007. The last quarter of 2007 was bizarre. With all avenues of raising cash from the market closing on us, I had to resort to borrowing from friends. Every day I would send text messages to friends from my phone's contacts database. I would be frank. I would say that we were in dire straits as a family and a Firm. That cash was critically needed to shore us up and prevent unlawful and illegitimate action against our family by both open market lenders and banks. I would seek the addressees' understanding and tell them not to call back or bother replying if they felt they did not either want to help or could not help.

One of the recipients of that message was Prateik. I must confess I thought a lot before sending that message to Prateik. Did I want to ask someone whom I had once sacked, rather ungraciously – for money? Would he give it to me? What would he think of me? And then, succumbing to the desperate situation, I pressed 'send' on my mobile phone.

Prateik landed up at the office within two hours of my messaging him. He insisted that my accountant patch him through to me on the phone as I was out – negotiating and buying time with banks and other creditors.

Prateik said, when my accountant put the call through, "AVIS, I have 15K (₹15,000 or $300) that I can spare. Please take it if it will help you."

I was humbled and dumbfounded at the same time. I said, my voice choked with emotion, "You? Prateik, you? Thank you so much. Please accept my apologies for what I did to you…"

Prateik cut me off. He said, "AVIS, please don't say anything. I am like the squirrel in Ramayana that makes a small contribution to Lord Rama's journey to Sri Lanka to bring Sita back.[20] I am blessed to be a part of your Life's journey."

---

[20] In the Hindu mythological epic Ramayana, a squirrel that was a devotee of Lord Rama, felt it could not carry the huge rocks that the monkeys were mobilizing to build a bridge to Sri Lanka. And so it carried small pebbles and dropped them in the spaces between the rocks. Rama, seeing the squirrel's dedication, carried it in his palm and fondled its back by running three of his fingers on it. Which is why, as the legend goes, squirrels have three stripes on their backs even today!

He didn't allow me to speak anymore. He said he had to rush back to work. My accountant later told me that he thrust the cash in her hand and rushed away.

I sent an email to Prateik thanking him. He did not reply. I kept him updated each quarter, just as I did with all creditors and friends who had helped us with their understanding and support. Prateik hardly replied. Nor did he even once ask for his money back. In fact, we still owe him that amount. In 2009, he sent me a Facebook friend request. I normally never add professional contacts on Facebook. Yet Prateik is the only such person whom I have added on Facebook!

I find a teacher in him, though he embarrasses me by claiming otherwise. He has taught me to forgive and understand people better. In my firing him, he claims, he learned what not to do and to develop a powerful work ethic. But what I have learnt most from him is that we must earnestly focus on understanding rather than interpreting people. It is easy to interpret my action in firing him: an arrogant perfectionist boss who refuses to give a fresher another chance. And perhaps I was really that person. But Prateik understood the opportunity hidden in the firing. That *he* had to change the way he worked if he had to achieve something. Then by coming back and connecting with me he understood the value of developing relationships, even if it was with an ex-boss who had been harsh on him. He refused to interpret me that way and gave our relationship a new beginning. Then again, when as a harried fellow-voyager through Life, I sought help, he understood the pain that I was going through and selflessly stepped forward, contributed and stepped back silently!

Several people on Facebook, close friends too, often tell me that given our bankrupt circumstances I must not give an impression that I am happy. One of them told me, "AVIS, people get the idea that you are happy living off other people's money!" But not Prateik. He wrote to me saying, "I am very happy to see you happy, Sir. Only when you are happy can you create value. And only by creating value can you come out of the crisis you and your family are in."

Today, on Teacher's Day, Prateik called me. I foolishly believed he was calling me about the money. And so I didn't take his call. Instead, I sent him a text, as I normally do to any creditor who calls, saying that things are getting delayed and that there is no change in our situation. Prateik replied, "Sorry to have disturbed you on a Sunday. Today is Teacher's Day. And I wanted to thank you for teaching me the importance of a sound work ethic, something that has helped me in the last 13 years. You are my *Guru* and I will always remain your student."

I want you both to imbibe this learning that Prateik has imparted to me. Prateik is an evolved human being. He understands an important truth – that your circumstances cannot impact your happiness, unless you allow them to. He refuses to interpret because he refuses to judge. Therefore, perhaps, he understands. Because he understands, he cares deeply. How lovely would it be if we could all, always, just understand and care for each other?

The problem with us is that we try to interpret everything. She said this – why? He did this – what does he want? If AVIS is asking for money – he deserved this plight; after all, he fired me unreasonably, didn't he? If Prateik is calling me – it must be to ask for his money back. Each of these is an interpretation of an event. When we interpret, we are busy intellectualizing each event. We are therefore, unable to *feel* the potential of the human being in us, or in others, in that moment!

There's this story of the old tramp, which Osho, the Master, used to narrate:

He stood at the back door and the lady of the house appeared.

"Lady," he said. "I was at the front..."

"You poor man!" she exclaimed. "One of the war victims. Wait till I get you some food and you can tell me your story. You were in the trenches, you say?"

"Not in the trenches," said the tramp. "I was at the front..."

"Don't try to talk with your mouth full, take your time. What deed of heroism did you do at the front?"

"I knocked," he said. *"But I couldn't get an answer, so I came around to the back."*

We are all like that lady. We don't even listen to the whole sentence. We listen to one word and start interpreting it. "The front..." and immediately you have interpreted – the war, the trenches, the war victim!

Life never tries to appeal to your intellect or mine. It only, always, animates our intuition. Raindrops falling on the ground, the chatter of the birds, the clouds in the sky, the fresh breeze that caresses your skin when you open the window, all these are Life's way of pulsing through your intuition. 'I am getting wet', 'The birds are noisy', 'The clouds are dark' and 'It's hot outside' – are your interpretations because you have intellectualized the experience.

The problem with and for all humanity is that we **interpret** and don't **understand**. Each of us is guilty of this. To cure many of the problems that we are confronted with, we must strive to **understand** each other, as humans, and not rush to **interpret**.

Don't Interpret, Understand!
Dad

5

Hello Millionaire!

"Kabir So Dhan Sanchiye, Jo Aage Ko Hoye
Sees Charaye Potli, Le Jaat Na Dekhya Koye"

Translation

"Kabir: Save the wealth that 'remains' in the
moment ultimate.
Departing with a crown of material wealth,
none has crossed the gate."

~ Kabir,
15th Century Weaver, Mystic, Poet

Friday, September 12, 2008
11 PM: Visakhapatnam

Dear Aash and Aanch,

Someone called me a millionaire today! And no, it wasn't a case of mistaken identity.

Aash, just last night you left for the United States, to start a new Life at the University of Chicago. As I left home this morning to travel to Visakhapatnam, I wondered how the house could look so different, feeling the way I was, knowing that you were not going to be here anymore. I was still thinking of you when I was checking in at the airport!

That's when Uncle R. U. Srinivas, whom we all fondly call RU, slapped me on my back. You may have met him on a couple of occasions at a mall or a movie.

He said, "AVIS, my dear, dear friend! You look like a millionaire! What radiance. You are exuding positive energy!"

I smiled and then laughed at his expression. I insisted, "RU, you must be joking. Millionaire? Me? I am broke and you know it."

Holding his gaze steady and looking me in the eye, Uncle RU declared, "As they say in cricket, my friend, form is temporary, class is permanent. To me, you were, are and will always be a millionaire!"

Knowing RU, and how genuine he is, I knew he had no reason to fake his sentiments. Besides, RU had helped us with cash when we were in dire straits and he hasn't ever asked for it. I reflected on his words. Here we are, a million dollars down, with no money to run the family. I knew we had to pick up a payment from this client in Visakhapatnam if Aanch's school fees' deadline was to be met later next week. And RU says that I look like a millionaire? Incredible!

Uncle RU's expression refused to leave me. I realized that we must not go by the current reality of what lies around us and outside us. Go within and what lies inside you is the Universe!

Many a times we get disheartened with our external environment. Look at the current recession. Consider our debt. Every client we approach claims there is no budget. And there's a million dollars to be paid back. The inability to secure any employment so that we could get some steady monthly income – yes, *Mom* and I floated our resumes more than once in the last 14 months but did not get any acknowledgement, forget a response, from recruiters – can be disheartening, to put it mildly. Maybe, the truth is this: no one wants to recruit failed entrepreneurs.

Rejection can debilitate us. In those times it is perfectly normal for you, and me, to imagine and perhaps conclude that we are worthless. That there is no hope for us. But that's totally untrue. Who you are is very different from what circumstances you are placed in. When you know who you are, you will discover the God within you and you will, for the first time, believe in yourself. That belief is all that is needed by the Universe to usher in a new set of circumstances to change your current reality for the better! This is not rocket science. This is not philosophy. This is the simple, real, truth! So, never let anyone – not you, not Life – tell you that you can't make it, that you can't achieve your dreams, that you are a failure or that you can't succeed.

I looked back at the face in the mirror in my hotel room this evening and said, "Hello Millionaire!" Because that's who I really am! I have learnt that you don't have to have money to be a millionaire. You can be rich in love, laughter, abundance, energy and, most of all, bliss! And I guess we are blessed with all of these as a family. The 11 movies we watched, over as many days, in September, before you left for Chicago, from the brilliant *Rock On!!,*[21] to the slapstick *Singh is Kinng,*[22] to the gripping *Sa-Ro-Ja,*[23] represents the ability we have to *live* fully, despite our circumstances. So what if we don't have money? As Uncle RU pointed out, we are millionaires nevertheless! And even in the practical sense, if we have to pay back a million bucks, in any case we had better make a few million more. So, we are millionaires, right?

Hello millionaires – to you both, to *Mom*, and to me…!

To My Little Millionaires,
Dad

---

[21] *Rock On!!* – a 2008 Hindi film directed by Abhishek Kapoor.
[22] *Singh is Kinng* – a 2008 Hindi film directed by Anees Bazmee.
[23] *Sa-Ro-Ja* – a 2008 Tamil film directed by Venkat Prabhu.

6

What Goes Around Comes Around

"If you knew what I know about the power of giving, you would not let a single meal pass without sharing it in some way."

~Gautama Buddha,
Buddhism Founder (563 BC ~ 483 BC)

Saturday, June 9, 2012
11 PM: Chicago

Dear Aash and Aanch,

C an *Mom* and I ever forget today? Or can either
    of you? My heart overflowed with gratitude
    watching Aash walking at his graduation,
along the Main Quad[24], amidst the University of
Chicago's iconic buildings. I am sure *Mom* felt the
same way because every time we looked at each
other during the day's celebrations and events,
our eyes welled up.

Of course, we are proud of you, Aash. Your ability,
despite being a Chennai-bred boy, to come here
and adjust to the insanely harsh Chicago winters,
is indeed commendable. Further, you managed
the GPA that you did despite the University of
Chicago's insistence on a questioning, seeking
spirit, absolute originality and wild creativity at all
times! Indeed our chests swell with pride. We also
remain grateful and will stay eternally indebted
to all those wonderful human beings who have
contributed so much to our lives in the last four
years of your under-graduate studies, making
today's graduation possible.

Who do we thank first? Who all do we thank?
So, many people have helped us! Voluntarily

---

[24] Main Quad – the quadrangle around which the University
of Chicago's buildings stand, in Hyde Park, Chicago.

at times, upon request at other times and just miraculously at so many other times. I did talk about some of them at the dinner at Vermilion[25] Restaurant hosted by Veena *chitti*[26] and Mahesh *chittappa*[27] this evening. Of course, we wouldn't have seen you graduate today without their 'big, huge, generous, spontaneous, voluntary last mile support'. Words cannot describe how indebted we feel to them. Or how we feel about the Universe's grace and miraculous energy that envelopes our lives – all our hotel stays on this trip have been paid for by redeeming points from the Starwood Preferred Guests' (part of Starwood Hotels) loyalty program, of which I am a member! It's amazing! Incredible.

Now let me go back to the question that many people, including Veena *chitti* and Mahesh *chittappa*, have asked in the past and am sure will continue to ask in the future: **Why, why in our right minds, would Mom and I let Aash go to the University of Chicago, when we were bankrupt and did not know how we would survive as a family, let alone pay a $60K plus tuition fee to the University?**

Good question. Pertinent. And it is not one that *Mom* and I did not ask ourselves.

---

[25] Vermilion – an Indian-Latin American fusion cuisine restaurant in Chicago (and New York).

[26] '*Chitti*' – means aunt, in this context, mother's sister, in Tamil.

[27] '*Chittappa*' – means aunt's husband in Tamil.

Actually, when Aash came to me with his University of Chicago application forms in June 2007, I remember telling him, "Son, if you are dreaming big, dream of getting into Harvard or Wharton or Stanford. The University of Chicago? I am disappointed."

Aash protested, "But *appa*,[28] the University of Chicago is *THE* University for Economics in the world."

The truth is I had **not** heard of the University of Chicago until then and my view of education in the United States was limited to Harvard, Wharton and Stanford. Besides, I always felt, Economics can be studied at Viveka or Loyola[29] in Chennai, or if you must, at St. Stephen's,[30] New Delhi.

Another reason why I hadn't paid much attention to Aash's aspirations or choice of college was because I was consumed with raising cash on a daily basis. All through 2007, we did not get a single engagement from clients despite sending out 180 proposals to as many companies in the same year. So, our Firm's already grave financial situation had ballooned into an unmanageable, towering, insurmountable mountain of debt. My daily routine involved showing bank statements to potential financiers, raising cash and paying off EMIs which had become due

---

[28] *'Appa'* – means father in Tamil.
[29] Viveka/Loyola – refers to Vivekananda and Loyola, respected colleges in Chennai.
[30] St. Stephens – a reputed college in New Delhi.

or overdue. So, Aash's University education was a bridge that I had intended to cross when 'we got to it'!

But then on Saturday, December 15, 2007, Aash's admission letter from the University of Chicago arrived. It is the most overwhelming and gratifying letter that a parent can receive. It made *Mom* and me resolve that come what may, Aash was going to Chicago.

Aash asked me that evening, "Dad, I understand your business is strained. I see you and *Mom* are so tense these days. I wonder if we can afford the University of Chicago fees."

I replied, "Son, you have done your job. You have secured admission to the best school for Economics in the world. Now let us do our job in working towards getting you in and keeping you there."

That statement was made out of bravado; it was not based on rational thought. Little did I know or realize then that our Firm would be declared bankrupt in every practical sense (even if not legally) and we would be insolvent, cashless and broke as a family, in just another fortnight!

Nevertheless, Aash went on to focus on his final year of high school in India. Aanch, you were busy with school as well, and I don't think either of you even realized the magnitude of the decisions *Mom* and I were taking at that time. *Truth be told, neither did we!*

It was never going to be easy. As we clawed out of absolute pennilessness to getting our daily, and then weekly, living expenses on track, we would often be stumped by a legal twist here or a hostile financier's threats there. Sometime in March 2008, *Mom* and I sat down and asked ourselves: "Can we really, humanly, support Aash's education in the US[31]?" The practical, logical answer was a no-brainer: **No. No. No!**

It is at times such as these that you place your trust and belief in a Higher Energy. This is what they call 'unwavering faith'. *Mom* and I had been long time followers of Shirdi Sai Baba,[32] and at that time, to a limited extent of Sathya Sai Baba[33] as well. Shirdi Baba's two point doctrine of 'Faith and Patience' particularly appealed to me. Intuitively, *Mom* and I both felt that Aash would not have been granted admission to the University of Chicago, if he was not destined to graduate from there. In order to ratify our 'gut feel' and 'belief' we turned to a father-son astrologer duo, Balan Nair and Ramamohan Nair. They were both respected for the accuracy of their predictions and for being no-nonsense, no mumbo-jumbo folks. We had been consulting with them since 2004 and they have been brilliantly accurate. Both of

[31] US/USA – the United States, the United States of America.
[32] Shirdi Sai Baba – an Indian Saint who lived in Shirdi, Maharashtra, a Western Indian state, between 1838 and 1918.
[33] Sathya Sai Baba – an Indian spiritual teacher and a soul-mate of Shirdi Sai Baba, who lived in Puttaparthi, Andhra Pradesh, a South Indian state, between 1926 and 2011.

them, individually, said two things: 1. Aash was destined to study away from home, in the West, and 2. His education would *NOT* be affected by our bankruptcy. *We, simply, believed in them and what they had to say, unquestioningly.*

Yet, with each passing day, the countdown was ticking away deafeningly: the US Visa interview, the initial fee payment, booking the flight ticket and the actual departure date. The stress was unbearable and it often got to me. I remember two occasions on which I almost changed my mind on letting Aash go. Both times it was *Mom's* leadership and decisiveness which won the day.

The first time it happened was on Sunday, June 15, 2008. I woke up as usual, at 4 AM, and woke *Mom* up too. I told her that with the limited visibility we had with our business, I was not sure we would be able to mobilize the funds at the right time for all of Aash's pre-departure financial commitments. I even questioned Aash's choice of University because it was so expensive and beyond our immediate reach. *Mom* argued with me, presenting the view that I must learn to be decisive.

She said, "You can either have faith. Or not. You can't have faith half-way. If we trust Baba[34] and also trust both Balan Nair and Ramamohan Nair,

---

[34] Baba – refers, in Vaani and AVIS' case, to both Shirdi Sai Baba and Sathya Sai Baba, as they see both as embodiments of a Higher Energy and grace in their lives.

we must be firm and believe that if all things fall into place, we can let Aash go. You can't keep going to Baba's temple or keep consulting the Nairs and still let your fears consume you."

I said that while I respected her sane perspective immensely, I felt it was only right we told Aash how grave our situation was so that he would not feel disappointed if things did not fall into place the way we hoped they would. *Mom* agreed. She however asked me to give Aash an opportunity to share his Vision for himself and how a University of Chicago education fitted in with that Vision. I thought it was a great idea. So we, Aash, *Mom* and I, decided to have the discussion in Coffee World on CPR Road[35] later that morning.

I began the discussion by saying, "Son, we really want to share with you what we feel about your choice of going to the University of Chicago. And want to tell you a few things you should know. But first let's hear you talk. What is your endgame? What's the idea behind pursuing Economics and why at the University of Chicago?"

Aash replied in his characteristic expressive, expansive way.

He said, "Guys, thanks! I agree we haven't really had this conversation. You will therefore please bear with me while I bring my sentiments

---

[35] Coffee World on CPR Road – a coffee place on C P Ramaswamy (CPR) Road, a commercial and residential area in South Chennai.

and thoughts to answering your questions. I feel half the world lives deprived and dependent. And if something, something at all must be done to make these people economically independent and self-sufficient, then a new economic order must be introduced. I am not sure what this order is or how it will work, but I am pretty sure only an economic solution can change the lives of half the world's people and I sense that I may be able to contribute to finding that solution. This is why I want to study the subject at the world's best school for Economics..."

Aash was still speaking when both our mobile phones beeped. *Mom* and I got distracted. With Aash's voice now in the background, I read the message. It was a message from our client, and now close friend, Anuja Kale Agarwal which had been sent to both our phones.

The message read: "Did you hear of Sumir's son?"

Uncle Sumir Anand, as you both know, is another client and again a very close friend. In fact, Uncle Sumir had helped us out with some cash in 2007 when I had reached out to him. Something, it appeared, had happened to his son, Curran, who was just two years younger than Aash. Aash, of course, knew him and was connected with him on Facebook. But I didn't interrupt Aash, who was still speaking.

Quietly, while still listening to Aash, I replied to Anuja's message asking: "No. What about him?"

Even as Aash continued to speak, though aware that *Mom* and I were a bit distracted, my phone beeped again.

It was Anuja's reply: "Curran was killed in a car crash last night in Gurgaon. A case of drunken driving by the driver of the car he was in."

I looked at *Mom*. I passed my phone to her. She read, her jaw dropping first and eyes filling next. Aash looked surprised. I broke the news to him. He was horrified and did not know how to proceed with the case he was making for himself. After discussing this extremely disturbing development with *Mom* for a few minutes, and vowing to find out more details soon, I turned to Aash.

I said, "Son, you are going to Chicago, if you get the Visa. Go, follow your Vision. We are very proud of you."

Indeed I was very proud of his Vision for himself and his wish to make the world a better place. On another day, another time, had we not been interrupted by the grave news of Curran's passing, I would have wanted to hear you Aash, sketch out your full Vision for yourself – without constraint, without restraint.

Both *Mom* and I gave Aash a hug and we got into our car in silence. As we rode home, I am sure all three of us felt pain and grief for Sumir and Gitika. Curran was their only child. We loved Curran too. He had grown up playing with Aash when they used to live in Chennai. I could feel the tears roll down my cheek as I turned into our building. As I walked up the stairs to our apartment, only one thought played on my mind. Here I was, with no money, but I had my son. And tragically, there was my dear friend Sumir, with all the money he had been saving up for Curran, but no Curran.

It was very clear in my mind: *Aash was going if he got his Visa.*

But the human mind is a monkey. Every time it finds a reason to jump, it will jump!

The second time I reconsidered the decision to send Aash to the US was in the wee hours of Wednesday, July 9, 2008, the day of Aash's Visa interview. I was on a client assignment at the Crowne Plaza Hotel in New Delhi. After completing my workshop for the day on Tuesday, July 8th, I had returned to my hotel room and sent an email to a client in Florida[36]. This is a client who had been in talks with us over the past three months and whose contract would cover our commitments to pay for Aash's University of Chicago fees. We had finished the contractual negotiations over the previous three weeks and we had been awaiting the final contract documents and were preparing ourselves for an eventual engagement kick-off. In my email to them I had asked if they had dispatched the final contract papers and if we could kick-off the project the following week.

---

[36] Florida – in the United States

I normally sleep soundly. Yet, around 2 AM on July 9th, I woke up sweating, although the air-conditioning was working just fine in my room. I sat at my computer and checked my email. To my horror, the client from Florida had replied saying they were deferring the contract because they had a new set of priorities to deal with internally!

I remember my heart started thumping faster as the implications of the contract not coming through sank into me: *Aash cannot go to the University of Chicago.*

I paced up and down the aisle in my room between the window and the door. I must have paced several thousand times. I was waiting for daybreak to call *Mom*. Why spoil her sleep, I thought? Let her sleep. Anyway, we had to accept and deal with this reality. During my endless walking spree, I further reasoned that it was impossible to get Aash to Chicago. Unknown to Aash, we had sourced an application form of Loyola College in Chennai, and I was convinced that form had to be used now. I wanted *Mom* to wake up to tell her that it is best we tell Aash it wasn't happening and tell him *not* to appear for the Visa interview that morning. Besides, to me at least, our documentation for the Visa application appeared to be woefully inadequate. I feared that the Visa may not come through.

As dawn broke over India, and outside my hotel window as New Delhi became noisier, I woke up

Mom. She heard me out and said, very matter-of-factly, "Fine *Dad*. So, we don't have the contract we wanted. But Aash will go if he gets his Visa. I have faith in Baba. I trust the Nairs. So, just relax and get yourself some sleep before your flight later today."

Her unruffled state of mind contrasted sharply with the turmoil I had been experiencing through that unforgettable night. She inspired me. And I too believed.

At 11.30 AM on July 9th, Aash came charging out of the US Consulate in Chennai, ran along the pavement towards Church Park school, took a right on Lloyds Road, and looked for our car and *Mom*. *Mom* had been waiting for the last two and a half hours in the car, praying. She had been texting me to be calm, promising me she would call as soon as she saw Aash. Now, upon sighting Aash, she called my number. She put her phone in speaker mode.

In my hotel room in New Delhi, I could hear Aash's voice, first distant and then drawing near, and nearer, screaming, "*Mom*, hey *Mom*, they gave me the Visa! I got the Visa!"

None of us could believe this was real. But it was.

Aash said, "The University of Chicago documentation and my high school records, convinced the officer that I was eligible. The officer congratulated me on getting into one of the best schools in the US and wished me well. And that was it. It took less than a few minutes!"

That's how Aash's journey to Chicago began and that's how it came about. I would have killed it twice with my fears, practical thinking or whatever, and both times *Mom* saved the dream by believing and by being decisive.

Yet, getting Aash to his campus and dorm in Chicago, as we were soon to discover, was the most minor of the many challenges we were to face. Over the next 48 months, each re-negotiated deadline with the University and each fee payment was a miracle. Each wire to Aash's travel card for his pocket and living expenses was a sign of the Universe's benevolence. To be sure, the University's partner, an outsourced firm that allowed parents to break up the fees due into six or eight monthly instalments, was a boon. But what do you do when even the committed fees, which were committed basis planned cash-flows, are not met because the cash just did not flow? Or because there was simply no cash! Hence, all these 48 months, Aash's account status with the University's outsourced partner was almost always delinquent. *Yet each time, Aash's University tenure came near a precipitous point, something, someone, somehow, as if an unseen hand was holding the strings up for Aash, for us, would come and bail us out.* It may sound bizarre. It may seem improbable. But this is what happened, every single time.

I remember one such time vividly. It was our 20th wedding anniversary on Tuesday, February 10, 2009. As usual, we were terribly short of money. I had just wired $500, out of a client payment, to

Aash for his living expenses. We had three months of fees outstanding to the University as per the committed payment plan. A sum of $6,700 was overdue. A fourth month of default would mean suspension from the University for Aash. We had no visibility at all, either of a new client or any overdue payments to us coming through because there was no payment overdue! We were also tormented by the fact that we had not managed to pay back our creditors, including family and friends, from whom we had borrowed money in 2007, promising we would be able to repay them in a quarter.

In a bankruptcy, as in Life, we have learnt, hope is both a good and a bad thing. It is good because you never want to give up thinking that things will eventually turn around. And bad because whatever you plan never really happens. So, if you borrowed money, being hopeful of returning it in three months, or even three years, you cut a sorry figure when you are unable to repay. There was no way we could borrow anymore from anyone to pay Aash's University dues.

That evening, Veena *chitti* and Mahesh *chittappa*, who were visiting India from Phoenix, Arizona,[37] insisted they wanted to take us out to dinner at The Lotus, a Thai restaurant at The Park, Gemini Circle[38] in Chennai. I was so preoccupied with the

---

[37] Phoenix, Arizona – in the United States.
[38] Gemini Circle – a famous landmark in the heart of Chennai, where the famous Gemini film studios once stood.

challenge of meeting the outstanding fees; I just did not want to go. But since they were in India and because I could not afford to buy *Mom* and Aanch dinner to celebrate the occasion, I accepted their invitation.

As we sat and ordered dinner, and as everyone around the table laughed and joked, *Mom* and I stared at our plates; occasionally pretending to like a joke or ask a question or pass a comment. *We thought it was all over for Aash.* That's when my phone rang. It was our client, Dr. Muhammed Majeed, the Chairman and Managing Director of Sami Labs,[39] whom I will refer to as Doc, calling from Bengaluru. The time was 9.45 PM. 'Doc? At this hour?' I remember wondering as I excused myself from the table to take his call.

"Hey AVIS! What are you up to, *maan*?" Doc thundered over the phone, in his inimitable Malayalam[40]-soaked American accent.

I replied in general terms. Doc had helped us personally with cash in the past when he came to know of our bankruptcy through one of his colleagues. So, I also told him things were bad and that we were still stuck for business and cash.

"AVIS, I want you down here. Let's talk, *maan*," he said.

---

[39] Sami Labs – a high-end research facility that develops and supplies Ayurvedic extracts for the global cosmetic, pharmaceutical and nutraceutical industry.
[40] Malayalam is the language spoken in the South Indian state of Kerala.

I told him I would fix up time with his office and come over on my next visit to Bengaluru. But Doc said he wanted me there the very next day. When I told him I didn't have money to buy the tickets, he admonished me for thinking that he expected me to pay for it. He said he would have the tickets purchased online in the next hour and that he wanted me to meet him first thing in his office the next morning.

Mom and I really didn't know what this was all about. We felt I must go because Doc has been very good to us. So, I arrived in Bengaluru the next morning. Doc's personal chauffeur was at the airport to receive me in a Mercedes Benz. I reached his office and was immediately ushered into his corner office. It must have been 10 AM when I entered. All the way till 3 PM, five hours on the trot, we remained undisturbed. All we did was talk management subjects: leadership, decision-making, people management, innovation and executive coaching. We had lunch together. And cups and more cups of green tea. Every hour, we stepped onto a beautiful balcony, and while Doc sat on an ornate swing and smoked, I walked about the greenery while talking to him at the same time. During the day, *Mom* texted me wanting to know what this trip was all about. I remember replying I had no idea what this was about and what I was doing there.

Then, at 3 PM, I told Doc that I must leave in the next 30 minutes, because my flight was at 5.30 PM.

Doc replied, "Sure. Yes. You must leave."

Then, almost as if, he had suddenly remembered something, he asked, "So, tell me AVIS, how can I help you and Vaani?"

I replied thanking him profusely for his kindness and said I really could not expect or accept any more help from him because we were already indebted to him.

But he cut me off and said, "AVIS! Do you think I am a fool to fly you down and spend a full day with you leaving aside all my work? Let me tell you that I was doing my *Namaaz*[41] in the evening yesterday and suddenly your face flashed in front of my closed eyes and I understood it was a sign from *Allah* to me to help you. That's why I called you. So, tell me how can I help you?"

Though surprised, intrigued and overwhelmed, all at the same time, I said again I couldn't think of anything.

Doc, who knew Aash was in Chicago, asked me, "How's your son? How are you meeting his University commitments?"

I replied, "He's fine but the truth is I am **not** meeting his University commitments!"

Doc sat up. He asked me for the exact amount. When I told him $6,700 was outstanding, he said, "Just send the account details to me over email when you get into Chennai this evening and

---

[41] '*Namaaz*' – a Muslim prayer ritual, done five times daily.

consider it done. Today, during business hours in the US, the wire will reach your son's University account from my personal account. You can repay me when able."

I wept when he told me that. I held his hand, looked in his eyes, and wept.

Embarrassed perhaps by my display of raw emotion, Dr. Majeed walked me to the door and said, "Come on AVIS! We are all human beings sent here to help each other. Now get going *maan*, you are late for your flight!"

Sure enough that night, India time, as *Mom* and I slept peacefully, the money went into Aash's University account, unknown even to him at the time!

This is just one instance, but this has happened every single time. With humbling consistency.

At one time it was a professional acquaintance from Sri Lanka, whom I met on a flight, who volunteered to give us a grant covering one month's fee. His only condition: "Continue the chain of goodwill and make Aash continue this chain so that it never stops!"

At another time it was a preference share investor whose investment we could not repay. I had sent him an update on email citing our grave circumstances. He called up to enquire about the family's welfare and said he had survived through a tough time himself and assured me all would be well. When he heard about Aash, he wired me the money for that month's fee.

We didn't always seek our benefactors. They walked into our lives unannounced, helped and stepped back. *It was as if they were ordered to do so and we were ordained to receive.*

The few times we asked, people helped spontaneously.

An industry stalwart based in New York responded to my request for a loan saying, "You don't have to take it as a loan, AVIS. Take it as an investment in the next generation from me. The University of Chicago is a premium school and if your son is studying there, be sure he is destined to do big things. This is my investment in him."

In another instance, Aash you will recall, we approached an entrepreneur, who is also a former client of ours, whose family runs an educational Trust[42] that supports deserving students with loans. When we asked him for help, the entrepreneur called Aash, who was in India during a summer break, over for coffee. Once convinced, he ordered his Trust's office to wire the money just in the nick of time.

And, yes, in his second year, thanks to an exceptional policy change made by Chase Bank, Aash secured a full year's tuition loan. However, this policy was not applicable to international students like him for their third and fourth years, and so, we were back to finding ways to raise cash

---

[42] Trust is an Indian corporate body, the equivalent of a Foundation.

or discovering the myriad ways the Universe had to express its generosity and kindness!

Last year, 2011, when Aash was here in India for the summer, we had a severe cash crunch again. A kind lady at the Bursar's Office at the University of Chicago, had been supportive of our situation and had been giving me reasonable deadlines and grace time, within the purview of the University's rules, each time I went back to her. She had, over these four years, developed a liking for Aash and our family. It was a relationship that we established over email. I transparently shared with her the challenges we were faced with and she always responded with understanding and great compassion. Yet, in September 2011, with an outstanding of over five months due for a previous year (2010~11), she warned me the Bursar will be forced to disallow Aash from resuming college for the next year (2011~12). I persisted. I wrote to her pleading with her to help us find a way. She directed me to contact the Bursar himself. I wrote to the Bursar laying our cards on the table, proposing a payment plan that went well beyond the first 90 days of the new academic year. I did not know him. I did not even know if he would be swayed by sentiment, because the outstanding was huge. But he reverted. Countering my proposition, he demanded that we pay, at 21-day intervals, equal instalments, with the first one starting on Friday, September 16, 2011. I received the Bursar's email on September 5, 2011. Less than a fortnight, and so much cash to be raised! I was worried. But the good news was the University would allow Aash to start his final and most crucial year at college if we could meet the September 16th deadline. We focussed on the brighter side of things. We had to comply with the first deadline!

A friend of mine, from my college days, who had been trying to reach me for months, called on September 6, 2011. I did not take his call. Instead, I texted him seeking his understanding saying I needed to focus on some things at my end.

He replied, obviously hurt, "Unless you want to avoid me totally, please call. What are friends for if we can't just pick up the phone and call each other?"

I called him back and told him I was sorry and confessed to being in a mess but I did not tell him what was occupying my mind, actually consuming me. He demanded I tell him.

When I did, he said, "Just this! Send me your account details. You will have the money tomorrow."

I didn't even think. I just sent him the account details. The money arrived on Wednesday, September 7, 2011.

Now, how do you explain this? You can explain this if it happened once. Maybe twice. Ok, maybe thrice. But numerous times over four years? To be sure, there were about 32 EMIs to the University of Chicago's outsourced payment plan partner to be paid over four years. Of these, eight instalments were taken care of by the bank loan in the second year. But between the first, third and fourth years, 24 instalments, had to be met. *And each time, they were met with the same pattern of a miraculous bailout happening in the very nick of time.*

Even Mahesh *chittappa's* call to me on the midnight of Saturday, May 26, 2012, just a fortnight ago, was inexplicable. While Veena *chitti* and Mahesh *chittappa* had helped us so many times financially over the last several years, *Mom* and I had decided we would not approach them for Aash's University fees. We felt indebted to them already and did not want them to be burdened any more. So, on the morning of May 26th, I wrote to them saying we were calling off our plans for coming to the graduation because the event itself may not happen for Aash. I cited our continued financial challenges and non-payment of fees as reasons for this decision. I know you were marked on that mail Aash and I know how strong you were through this decision. Mahesh *chittappa* spoke to me that night and said he could not see you not graduate after all this effort and convinced me and *Mom*, together with Veena *chitti*, that they trusted us and they believed that education is the biggest gift that can be given to anybody. It was an overwhelming phone call. I remember sitting with *Mom* through the rest of the hours of that night and crying intermittently but, often, inconsolably.

What did we do to deserve this generous treatment at the hands of the Universe? I have heard that God appears in human form. *If that is*

*indeed true, as we have come to believe, then we
have seen God, over and over again.*

It wasn't until the graduation got over this
afternoon and much until after dinner, after Aanch
and *Mom* have gone to sleep in our hotel room by
the Navy Pier here in Chicago, did it all become
clear to me. *I now know why we were helped by
the Universe. We were helped because what goes
around, comes around!*

Let me elaborate. In 1994 I used to work for
Business Today[43] magazine, in Bengaluru. Aanch,
you would be born only the following year. It was
just Aash, *Mom* and me in our Malleswaram[44] home
at that time. My monthly salary was ₹13,500 (about
$270) and I was writing stories on start-ups and
strategy for the magazine then. One morning, I
arrived early at work wanting to meet a deadline. As
I walked up to use the restroom, close to the pantry,
I noticed the housekeeper, a matronly lady called
Jayamma, crying silently. I paused and asked her
what the matter was. She said her son's school fees
were due and she did not know what to do. She
said she had to pay the fees by noon that day or
else, the school would suspend her son. Her boy, I
learned, was good at academics and the school was
a premium English-medium school. I found out that
her requirement was ₹750 (about $15) monthly. I

---

[43] *Business Today* – A business fortnightly from the *India
Today* (a leading weekly news magazine) stable.
[44] Malleswaram – a Bengaluru residential suburb.

pulled out my wallet; I had ₹1000 (about $20) with me then, and paid her ₹750. I told her to go pay the fees. She fell at my feet. I was just 27 then and I was embarrassed to the point of being angry.

I admonished her and remember telling her, "We are all human beings first. All of us are equal. Go pay the fees and tell your son to study well. My family will support yours until your son graduates and finds himself a job."

Over the next 12 years, till 2006, every month, we kept sending ₹750 without fail to Jayamma. We did so even after we moved out of Bengaluru in 1996. It was part of our monthly budget to send money to her. Occasionally, she would call me or *Mom* in Chennai and ask for more, citing a college admission fee or a clothing requirement for her son. From 2002, I stopped hearing from her but the money went into Uncle Deepak Pawar's (who is a photographer with *Business Today*) account monthly, and he would pay Jayamma and keep me posted. We maintained this commitment even as our lives became financially challenging since 2002. Some months, we even had to cut down expenses for you both, Aash and Aanch, to support Jayamma. Then one day in 2006, after receiving the remittance, Uncle Deepak called me. He said he had learned that Jayamma's son had got himself a job that paid him a five figure starting salary and that the boy was now capable of looking after his mother and that Jayamma did not need to be sent this money anymore.

I appreciated my former colleague's update. I also remember thinking that a simple thank you or an update from the boy to his benefactors, us, would have been in order. But then I expunged the thought, saying to myself that expectations always bring hurt.

Now, when I look back, I think the only reason we deserve to have been helped by the Universe and its wonderful people is because we helped Jayamma and her boy selflessly. Since then, *Mom* and I have continued to help people. Even during our darkest years, if we had some cash with us, and if we believed it could help a kid's education, we have supported that kid. Our logic has always been: *Treat someone's need as higher than yours, even if you don't have enough. Because your want may actually be someone's need.* I am not sure if I am right in my thinking, but I am sure *Mom* and I have done the right thing every time we have paid someone's fees even if we could not meet Aash's University commitments on time!

When you give – just give. Don't analyze. Don't expect anything, not even a thank you, in return. And don't give by holding back. Just give freely. Look at all that people have given us *without* expectations. *Without* wanting anything in return. Hafez, a 14th Century Sufi poet has said: 'Even after all this time, the sun never says to the earth, "You owe me". Look what happens with a love like that! It lights up the whole sky.' So, give yourself, of yourself, selflessly.

Who taught you to speak? Who taught you the alphabet? And the numbers? Who taught you to know you are human, you are capable and you can love? If you can read what I have written or access Facebook, it is a result of your ability to recognize and interpret a maze of characters and operate your fingers on a keyboard! None of what I describe has anything to do with your social strata or earning ability. All of this has been possible because someone, somewhere – parents, siblings, family, teachers, friends – gave you their time freely. So, giving need not be imagined as an act of giving away money to charity or to someone underprivileged. Give your understanding to someone who craves it. Give your time to those who need your counsel/support. Or give someone a warm, compassionate hug. Giving is the most beautiful part of being human.

I am glad *Mom* and I gave. And gave freely. For, when it was our turn to receive, the Universe too gave freely! Without giving we would not have known that what goes around comes around. We wouldn't have discovered what it means to be human!

Live, Love, Give!
Dad

7

You Can Never Get A Perfect 10!

"*It is easy to get everything you want, provided you first learn to do without the things you cannot get*."

~ Elbert Hubbard,
American Editor, Publisher, Writer (1856 ~ 1915)

Monday, May 4, 2009
11.45 PM: Chennai

Dear Aash and Aanch,

Today I have been charged with assaulting your grandmother, my mother, your Geetha[45] *paati!*[46] I am consumed by grief and shame.

My relationship with my mother is an unusual one. She's given birth to me, she's raised me and she's fought many a battle with Life for me and my siblings. I am, and will remain, grateful to her for these and other things she has done for me. Yet my mother and I have never bonded. I have tried to understand this but have never been successful. I do have a sense, now that I am over 40, of why we don't bond. My mother is a very ambitious person. I believe that to her, status, prestige and social standing are more important than running a family or home. She needs to see monetary gain or derive social privilege from whatever she does. To achieve these ends she can adopt, at times, even in dealings within the family, what appear to me to be, unfair means. Over a period of several years I have concluded that she is manipulative as well as possessive.

At least, this is how I feel about her.

---

[45] Geetha – AVIS' mother's name.
[46] *'Paati'* – means grandmother in Tamil.

These ethical conflicts have completely alienated me from her. Which should tell you both why you don't get to see too much of her in our lives or why in the times that you have seen us together, you have found us arguing, shouting and screaming. *I have concluded that the chemistry between us just does not work.* Of course, I came to this conclusion after much trial and error, after many attempts over several years, to find a common meeting ground for both of us ideologically, and failing.

Initially, I could not even comprehend why I differed from her on everything. In my years as a teenager, I dismissed this as me being plain rebellious. As I grew older and became a working professional, a husband and a father, I saw that the distance between us had actually become unbridgeable. Once, a few years ago, I attempted to bridge this distance between us by sitting her down and tried to make her understand how I felt about her. I told her how much I respected her for what she had done for me as a mother. But I also said that I could not accept her doing some things and the way she was doing them. It didn't have any impact on her though. The next day she accused me of trying to 'usurp' her position as head of the family!

During the years preceding our bankruptcy, I did, with some poor wisdom, and faulty logic, borrow money from my parents and even pledged the family property with a bank to raise cash. To be sure, all the money raised from this effort went to servicing our Firm's debt. Yet, we were unable to stabilize our Firm's finances with this or other methods. Eventually, I was not able to either return the money I had borrowed nor was I able to redeem the family property from the bank.

This evening my mother summoned me for a 'meeting' and declared that I was a 'cheat' and a 'defaulter'. She said she had come to that conclusion because we had decided to send you Aash, our son, to the 'elite and expensive' University of Chicago for your under-graduate studies and because I was flying around the country. I begged for her understanding and said, that we had sent our son in the hope that he will be able to arrange for his tuition fees through a bank loan or a grant or something and that I was flying for work and that clients were paying for the tickets. *(Dear Reader: Just for the record, in case you are reading this chapter in isolation, my son didn't get a grant and all his funding happened through miracles that the Universe manifested. More on that in an earlier chapter in this book.)*

My mother, as you both must know well by now, once she starts speaking, will go on and on, endlessly, without allowing anyone else to speak. Tonight she was incomprehensibly belligerent. She insinuated that we *have* the money and that we are *faking* a bankruptcy and *cheating* her and the family! I was upset. And I could feel the anger rising in me. In the 1975 classic, *Deewar*,[47] Amitabh Bachchan[48] made his presence felt in Indian cinema by displaying his angst each time he referred to a tattoo that someone had forced on him as a child. The tattoo in Hindi famously read: '*Mera baap chor hai*', meaning 'My father is a thief'. *I felt as much angst to be told repeatedly by my own mother that I was a cheat!*

I was shattered. And when she continued to berate my poor moral values in not honouring my word, I lost my cool and wanted to shut her up, so I could speak. I rushed to her, cupped her mouth and forced some silence into the room. She resisted me. Pushing me away, she howled that I was trying to assault her. I found her charge grave. I was struck by an unimaginable, heavy burden of grief.

I came home and wept in (your!) *Mom's* arms, and concluded that if things had to change, I had to change my attitude towards my mother. I decided to forgive her and forgive myself in the process. *I have decided that the best way to deal with the situation is for me to accept that while she is my mother, there really is no bond between us. And there never will be.* I will have to live with this acceptance that in my Life, there will never be a maternal influence. No warm, loving, caring feelings that all mothers have for their children.

---

[47] *Deewar* – meaning 'Wall', a Hindi film directed by Yash Chopra.
[48] Amitabh Bachchan – a Hindi movie legend and superstar.

I have come to accept that my mother will never trust me. That she will perhaps never believe that I am genuine, that I am a victim of circumstances and that I am working hard to both repay her and the family and redeem my credibility!

I guess, more than my mother's insinuation that I was a cheat, what hurt me was her effort to misunderstand me. She is my mother and I expect her to trust me when I say I have no money. Funnily enough, while my own mother chose not to trust me, many of our creditors have continued to trust us all these months and wait patiently for us to repay. However, I will live, ever grateful to my mother for having given birth to me, and for having raised me. I will live basking in the abundance of so much love, understanding and care that you both, your mother and the Universe shower on me!

You can never get a perfect 10 in Life! Something, somewhere will remain unfinished, unstuck and unresolved. It is an effort in futility if you try to fix all of what's wrong with your Life. You will feel frustrated, depressed and beaten down if you try to. Most of what you struggle with, suffer for, comes from your desire to fix these unfixable areas. And these areas are different for each person. Someone may never find a companion. Another may never find a job. Yet another may not have a resolution to a prolonged property issue. Someone else will have a perennial health problem. Or someone may just get no understanding from members of the family. In my Life, one of the unfixable areas is my relationship with my mother. Intelligence lies in knowing which parts of your Life you can fix and which parts you can't. Those you can fix, well, you don't need to grieve over them at all. And those that you can't fix, why grieve over them anyway?

Of course, you can never say you can't fix something unless you have tried. So, when you try but do not succeed, you need to let go. I have decided to let go. This is your learning too. You must focus only on those aspects of your Life that you can add value to. Live with the acceptance and understanding that there will be a few parts of your Life that will remain unresolved. This is not escapism. It is a simple, practical framework, in fact, to find peace and abundance in Life! This is a way of finding bliss – knowing what you have and knowing too what you will never have and in accepting both!

Peace,
Dad

8

Life Will Always Go On

"In three words I can sum up everything I've learned about Life: It goes on."

~ Robert Frost,
American Poet (1874 ~ 1963)

Tuesday, April 27, 2010
9.45 AM: Chicago

Dear Aash and Aanch,

Yet another miraculous set of circumstances have brought us to the US and to Chicago! Suddenly a client appears from nowhere. They want us to lead a four-day transformation program for their team in Iowa[49] on how to deal with 'uncertainty in these recessionary times'. They want *Mom* and me both on board. We ask them to pay for Aanch's tickets too as part of our fees and decide to dedicate the entire earnings to taking care of our visit to Chicago to be with you, Aash.

The last fortnight in the US and the last few days in Chicago have been a dream.

We have come and seen what a great decision it has been to send Aash here, to the University of Chicago, to study in one of the most enabling environments for fostering a questioning spirit and creative thinking. Beautiful minds teach and are taught here. The University looks so beautiful – from its heritage buildings to the seductive ivy on their walls.

Most important, we have come here and have seen how our wonder-boy, Aash, has become a

---

[49]   Iowa – in the United States

man. How the brutal winters have been conquered and how punctuality, discipline and a high-performance ethic have been inculcated and how an ownership of Life and career have been triggered awake in Aash's psyche. As a father this realization and going through this unique experience, this miracle, has been so rewarding, so humbling!

I have felt many a times that I have fallen short of what I could have done for both of you. In the early years of your childhood, I worked hard at earning a living. Then, as you both entered your adolescent years, I felt I was struggling with three constituencies at the same time: my Vision for our Firm to be an Indian consulting Firm that's respected globally, my responsibility towards your academic careers and my last-ditch attempts of saving our sinking Firm and our family! Indeed *Mom* has partnered in every decision I have taken and has stood by me, but I believe somewhere, I have indeed failed. Is this what I promised *Mom* when I married her? Is this what I had planned for you both when you were born? A *bankruptcy*! Of all things?

And yet, with nothing in hand, things that most people can only aspire to, are happening in our lives! Our lives, it seems, defying all logic, go on, as if run by remote control by a destiny-planner or a supercomputer or the Universe. It is soul-stirring. I feel poetry flow from within me. Let me attempt it:

Son,

As you turned away and walked last night,

Into the cold, windy, Chicago night,

I stood staring and then, reluctantly, started walking,

I paused, turned and looked for you down 57th street,

But you had walked farther away, a few more feet...

I just took in the cold air,

My lungs filled with pride,

A tear dropped and made the icy wind sting my cheek as it rolled down,

I turned around and resumed walking... away....

We were two men now,

Walking away from each other,

Because, I sighed smiling, such is the nature of Life;

The little boy who held my finger 19 years ago

Was now on the road... to Life, learning and love...

As we explored the University (of Chicago) campus today,

As the import of your new Life and times here sunk in,

As I looked at your Mom,

My love for her grew and glowed in me, in abundance...

What a beautiful Life, she had nurtured in you, so patiently, so lovingly,

In a manner that only she can...

At the C-Bench[50], in the Main Quad,

I saw you enthusiastically extol the acoustic virtues of the venue to your sister,

And my heart strings were tugged...

Such a beautiful friendship is Life's gift to parents

We are blessed, I said in gratitude, as I captured that moment for eternity...

The bells that tolled at the Rockefeller Chapel at noon, yesterday,

Made me fall in love with Mom, once more; perhaps for the trillionth time...

As I stood in the empty altar with hands on her shoulders,

Posing for a picture postcard portrait frame,

I felt how much more sensible it is to live, just live,

Than to worry,

For when you live and let Life take its own course,

You enjoy every moment soulfully... like this one...

There will soon be a time,

When we will experience your sister's Life,

Just the same way as we did yours today

---

[50] C-Bench – a gift from the Class of 1903 to the University of Chicago, it has special acoustic properties; if you stand in the centre of the C-Bench, facing the 1903 inscription, anything you say will be echoed back to you.

And feel the same sense of pride and joy,
And you will share in that pride too, I know...
And soon, son, you will write an ode to your child
and email us a copy
Reminding us that Life, like a beautiful heart, will
go on...
Dad

Practically, technically, theoretically, this trip could not have happened. Yet it has. We didn't seek it. We didn't know this client even existed! It was an opportunity that came to us because a satisfied client recommended us to them.

Just over a fortnight ago, on the afternoon of our departure to the US, *Mom* and I were in a courtroom in Chennai facing charges for financial default and a claim for a loan to be repaid. The judge wanted the next hearing to be posted for today and we knew this trip would be in jeopardy if the judge insisted. Because our presence in court was mandatory to avoid an *ex-parte* hearing, our lawyer convinced the judge to schedule the case for a later date and that's how we were able to leave India.

Interestingly, our flight into London from Chennai was delayed. Since we missed the connecting British Airways flight to Chicago's O'Hare Airport, British Airways put us up for a night in London. That was Aanch's first visit to London. We hired a taxi and saw London in a whirlwind tour through the night! Another miracle. Another example of the inscrutable, yet, wondrous ways of the Universe!

Now, at the fag end of this amazing US trip, I ask myself again if all this is **real**. *Mom* and I are broke, and yet there is so much abundance? We believe we are all indeed blessed.

The learning that I will take home is about Life itself. I realize that in the end it will all be fine. Every single thing. None of our stories, or lives, is going to have a messy, sorrowful ending. Let us not grieve or mourn in anticipation of a sad ending. Because, it is just not going to happen. Worries consume our thinking when faith is weak or disappears. Where worry abounds, fear lurks in the dark shadows. When fear looms, it is a clear sign that we have moved away from accepting Life for what it is, and are trying to 'wish' that our Life was different. This is the perfect breeding ground for low self-esteem and depression. Don't allow such insecurities to chew you up and weaken you. Perhaps it is time to take things as they come. Instead of wanting and wishing things were different. No matter what you wish, or what you want, Life will go on. No dark night can be avoided. And no darkness is permanent. In the end, light will shine on us, and bathe us in joy, peace, love and abundance. Life's like this only!

Zindagi, Kaisi Hai Paheli... Haaye...[51]
Dad

---

[51] *'Zindagi, kaisi hai paheli...haaye'* – An iconic Hindi song, a paean to the inscrutable nature of Life, sung by Manna Dey in Hrishikesh Mukherjee's 1971 classic *'Anand'* meaning 'Joy'.

9

Celebrate Life

"Celebrate what you want to see more of."

~ Tom Peters, Management *Guru*

Sunday, March 2, 2008
9 PM: Chennai

Dear Aash and Aanch,

Did you notice that I hardly ate when we all sat together at lunch today? It is Aanch's birthday tomorrow. Her 13th. And the celebrations began today.

What a miraculous lunch we had at Raintree Hotel, St. Mary's Road![52] It was overwhelming for *Mom* and me to see you both goofing around – laugh, pull each other's legs and bring in Aanch's birthday! We chose to do lunch outside today because all of us could be together only today; what with final exams for both of you and a working week beginning tomorrow.

I think in all the excitement, Aash and Aanch, you didn't notice that I was choking on my food, that I was fighting back my tears; that I hardly ate. And Aash, the super sharp observer that you normally are, didn't you realize that I never paid for lunch? Since it was just the four of us and Venks *thatha*, I should have been the one to pay in any case! The truth is there was no check and that we are in no position to have paid for lunch in any case!

---

[52] Raintree Hotel, St. Mary's Road – St. Mary's Road is a quiet neighbourhood in South Chennai.

Our meal was paid for by our dear friend, my mentor and legal counsel, Uncle Vijayaraghavan. It has been only two months since we engaged Uncle Vijayaraghavan professionally, though we have known him for over 20 years. He is an amazing human being, an extremely ethical professional and an exceptionally erudite, strategist-lawyer. He has been a pillar of support for *Mom* and me.

When *Mom* and I met him on December 31, 2007, and apprised him of our dire situation, he smiled and told us, "Let me tell you three things: 1. You are bankrupt, all right. But please know that the inability to repay people (because of circumstances) is **not** a crime. 2. Know also that you have to make meeting creditors, facing threats, often going to the police station or appearing in courtrooms, a part of your professional Life. It is your duty and you will not shirk it. 3. Never let your self-esteem and morale be affected. Remember this is a phase in Life and this too shall pass."

He also said that he would represent us in ALL legal matters and that he did not expect us to pay him any professional fees until we were able to.

"I trust you both. Remember, I don't ever bet on a lame horse," he exclaimed emphatically.

Meeting him and hearing these words made a huge difference to our morale. In the last few months Life has been about meeting creditors and begging for time or pleading with them not to harm the family or not to come home and create a scene. It has been about feeling miserable and having to do things that we don't like to do. *Humbling experiences are romantic and inspiring to hear about but extremely painful to go through. Mom* and I have been going through them while growing in humility and resilience.

Some creditors understand but they are few in number. Some are anxious. Some others are completely unreasonable. And a few try and terrorize you. One of them, a collection manager at a large financial institution, a person called Alankar,[53] had been calling our accountant, a young lady, at the office and threatening to send *goondas*[54] over to collect their dues. Initially, even I was petrified of his calls, based on what our accountant relayed to me. On December 31, 2007, I borrowed ₹30,000 (about $600) from a close friend to meet an overdue single EMI and reached it to Alankar's office just in time to avoid any precipitate action by him. When their January EMI was due, I went to Alankar's office with *Mom* and told him we would not be able to pay that month's EMI. Alankar did not even heed a plea for time.

He thundered to a colleague of his in Kannada[55] (a language Alankar thought we did not know,

---

[53] Real name not disclosed to protect identity.
[54] '*Goondas*' means goons.
[55] Kannada – a language spoken in the South Indian state of Karnataka.

though actually we did), "Tell this man to sell his wife's *thali*[56]and raise cash!"

Alankar's colleague was as horrified as we were, to see how Alankar was trampling on our dignity. He knew, just as we did, that the Reserve Bank of India's[57] guidelines for financial institutions disallowed such treatment of any defaulter. But who was to speak of the law to Alankar?

That's what had brought us back to Uncle Vijayaraghavan's office a few weeks ago. *Mom* and I were quite emotional when we recounted Alankar's behaviour to Uncle Vijayaraghavan. We also told him how scared we were. We did not know what awaited us the next hour. Every time the phone rang, each time the doorbell rang, I would panic and get into a high-alert mode. *Who was it? How do we manage this creditor? What if they assaulted us in their desperation to recover their dues?* As I shared these and more of my concerns with Uncle Vijayaraghavan, I must have looked defeated.

Indeed I was. Ever since January 2nd, the day offices opened after the New Year break, I had been going from financier to financier, bank to bank, lender to lender; meeting, sharing, and seeking people's understanding and time to repay. *Mom* accompanied

---

[56] *'Thali'* is a sacred thread, often made of gold, which South Indians, particularly, Tamilians, believe is the equivalent of a wedding ring.

[57] Reserve Bank of India, RBI, the Indian Federal Bank governing all banking laws and operations.

me to several of these meetings. We discovered that people were completely convinced of our genuineness. They had no doubt. In fact, several of them thanked us and appreciated our coming to them proactively instead of them having to chase us – which is normally the case with defaulters in India, they just disappear! Yet, none of the creditors was willing to give us time. They wanted their money. Period. When people are unwilling to relent or reconsider, you do feel defeated.

Uncle Vijayaraghavan sensed the despondency in both me and *Mom*. He smiled after both of us had finished narrating our harrowing experiences and asked us in his inimitable baritone, "AVIS, what is your favourite wine?"

Even as I fumbled, flummoxed by his asking about wine when we are talking about a Life-and-death situation, he looked at *Mom* and asked her, "And yours Vaani? Red or White?"

Both *Mom* and I were bewildered and did not know what to say.

Sensing this, he continued, "Listen Vaani and AVIS, the first thing is for you to know that you must not let any of this get to you. You can't look like this – deflated, defeated. Your morale must never get affected. Don't ever allow anyone to touch it. I want you both to go get a Life. Name your favourite restaurant, name your favourite wine. It's on me. Just go and unwind guys! Life is much more beautiful than you believe it is at this time!"

It was a generous and inspiring offer, from a very learned and experienced man. While we were touched, *Mom* even wept inconsolably for a while, we were too depressed to accept his offer. But he would have none of that. Finally, more as a way of closing the issue, so we didn't hurt a well-wisher, I said that we would take a rain check.

Today's lunch at Raintree, my dear children, was courtesy Uncle Vijayaraghavan. I called him up last week and asked him if I could exercise my rain check. And he spontaneously took charge. I was even more touched and humbled. He asked for the number of people and was a bit disappointed to know that we were not going to have wine. He personally went to the hotel and swiped an open authorization for the lunch ahead of our arrival so that we were not embarrassed.

I would never have called him but Aanch cuddled up to me a few days ago and asked me naively, "*Appa*, where are we going out to eat to celebrate my birthday?"

That's when the reality hit me – hard and inescapable. I realized little girls have starry-eyed dreams and a romantic view of Life. Little girls also like nice, cute things, and sometimes silly but precious wants which when fulfilled, fill you, the provider, with a sense of accomplishment that is both matchless and memorable. With her asking me this question with such innocent expectation, I felt stung by enormous guilt.

There are so many things that a girl seeks when she steps out of her childhood and discovers the woman in her and it is only the parent who can make her feel special.

I, on the contrary, felt that in the last couple of years I had deprived both of you in general and Aanch in particular, of all the things I would have wanted you to have. Not that your desires were extravagant or that you were spoiled. You both are very grounded and I am grateful to your *Mom* for keeping you that way. But you have to be a parent, a father, to understand the agony of not being able to even give your children things like a nice meal in a fine dine-in place on a special occasion or an iPod or a mobile phone or a new pair of shoes. Things that are normal these days for an upper middle-class family in India. Not that either of you has ever complained, but for me, the grief of not being able to do these things is palpable.

So, when Aanch asked me where we were celebrating her birthday this year, and I arranged it through Uncle Vijayaraghavan, it seemed like a mission had been accomplished, not simply that a normal annual celebration was happening. When all of us dined at lunch today and *Mom* smiled at the two of you having fun, I wept, swallowing the tears so you would not see them. And I was not grieving because we had no money. I was emotional because we didn't deserve this benevolence from the Universe.

Here are your *Mom* and *Dad*, paupers in every conceivable materialistic sense; yet we are the richest parents in the world! We have the wealth of a happy family, wonderful children and the benign presence of Venks *thatha* in our lives! We are celebrating Life in the most true, magical, miraculous manner. Our new world does not require us to transact with money – almost literally, because no check arrived at our table – Uncle Vijayaraghavan had taken care of it – yet it is full of abundance. If this is not the magic and beauty of Life, what is?

I have concluded that we must learn to separate ourselves from the situations that haunt, agonize and worry us the most. Ask yourself how you would feel if these situations did not exist. Invariably, you would answer that you would be in peace. So, just imagine that it is true – that those situations do not exist – and experience peace. And the rare state called bliss. Once you taste peace and bliss, you get addicted to it. You wouldn't want anything else.

I am not advising you to delude yourself. The truth is, what lies between you and inner peace are layers of worry, guilt, hatred, grief, and anger about situations that have happened or you imagine are waiting to happen. The present is always beautiful and peaceful. If you learn the fine art of peeling away those layers, you will become that peace.

Take for example, today's lunch, when we celebrated Aanch's birthday. What caused me agony? Was it our bankruptcy that was worrying me? Not really. What was upsetting me was the manner in which I, as a provider, had been rendered cashless and helpless, and the fact that the future was uncertain. The present, when we were at lunch, I had no problem with. And why would I? After all the lunch had been arranged for and paid for, despite our situation! Now, if the past and the future did not worry me, wouldn't I have been happier at lunch?

In fact, we – me, you – are happy, right now. Yet we all kid ourselves by imagining we are unhappy.

The simple truth to remember time and again is that you are inviting your suffering by letting the past haunt you and the future worry you. You have no control over either. If you employ basic common sense, intelligent living is all about what *is*. Happiness is a state that cannot be pursued or attained. You *are* the happiness you seek. You just need to accept that state. The Buddha taught us not to pursue the past because he wanted us to not grieve over what's over but to celebrate what *is*. So, peel away those layers that prevent you from being who you *are*. Don't worry. *Be* the happiness you seek!

My dear precious children, everything we need to celebrate Life is here with us now. We are alive. We are educated, we are not dying of starvation (the Universe, somehow, has provided for us in the past few months, and I am sure will continue to do so in the future), we have a home to go to, we are loved and are capable of loving. What more do we need to live? Money? *Nah*! Power? Position? Security? Give up all that you don't need, don't have, and keep pining for. **Live** with what has been ordained and is with you already. Witness then the magic and miracle of Life showering you with abundance!

Celebrate Life!
Dad

10

Follow Your Bliss

"Follow your bliss and the Universe will open doors where there were only walls and only you will be able to see those doors."

~ Joseph Campbell, American Mythologist
and Writer (1904~ 1987)

Tuesday, December 20, 2011
11 PM: Navi Mumbai

Dear Aash and Aanch,

*M*om and I wept today. They were tears of joy. We wept, I believe, because our decision to retool our business model, seven years ago, which accelerated our bankruptcy and threw all our lives completely out of gear, has finally been vindicated.

Something remarkable happened this afternoon. *Mom* and I are in Navi Mumbai. Today we finished the last of 30 workshops, which were part of an eight month 'culture transformation' project with a multinational client, whose India operations are head-quartered here. The CEO of this company, an IIT-IIM[58] professional, with 30 years in the paints and chemicals industry, is an inspiring leader. In his closing address to over 50 managers from his leadership and middle-management team, he celebrated *Mom* and me and gave us a citation for 'touching lives, making a difference and creating value for his team and the organization'.

He declared emphatically, "Associating with Vaani and AVIS is one of the most rewarding

---

[58] IIT – Indian Institute of Technology, the premier engineering school in India; IIM – Indian Institute of Management, the premier B-school in India; alumni are generally 'best-in-class' professionals!

decisions we have taken here and we have been enriched as an organization by the experience".

It was embarrassing no doubt to be eulogized, but overwhelming all the same.

Mom and I hugged each other when we got back to our hotel room and cried. Those tears were indeed an expression of boundless joy.

We were not merely elated over being felicitated by the CEO of a global company. This happens often with us. People do love us for the work we do and give us commendable testimonials, always without us asking for any. We were both moved and delighted because the project we had just completed was significant for three reasons: 1. It was the first purposeful, and the largest so far, project we had done that reflected our new, enhanced business model. 2. It had meant 63 days of engagement at premium billings. 3. Our premise and approach for transforming their culture was initially received with a lot of scepticism by the client and its people; so, to be celebrated at the end of the mandate meant that we had pulled off an incredible outcome.

When you fight such odds and endure all the pain that comes your way while you follow your dream, refusing to compromise with what gives you joy, and when someone *finally* tells you that you have created value, you have made a difference, it is a very humbling experience and a *beautiful* feeling. There's great joy in simply knowing that all of this has not been in vain. *That our business model works, as does our faith!*

In a time like this, I know that even if we died now, we would die in peace, in joy!

I am, in fact, reminded of the song from the 1969 super hit Rajesh Khanna-Sharmila Tagore-starrer 'Aradhana'.[59] Sung by the venerable Sachin Dev Burman, the original lyrics written by Anand Bakshi go like this: "...*banegi aashaa ek din teri ye niraashaa, kaahe ko roye, chaahe jo hoye, safal hogi teri aaraa-dhana, kaahe ko roye...*" Translated, it means: "...your despair will turn into hope, why do you cry, let whatever happens, happen; your prayers will be heard, your penance will be successful, why do you cry..."

But we are not ready to rest in peace yet. Not quite. *Because our financial recovery, and our debt repayment, is still to happen.*

There's a question we are always asked. And I am sure you may both ask that too, sometime soon. *Why did our Firm go bankrupt?* I never shy away from sharing why this happened. Therefore, *Mom* and I believe you should both know the answer to this question as well.

Let me begin with my upbringing and my evolution as a professional. You both know I come from a middle-class background. And though

---

[59] *Aradhana* – meaning 'Prayer', a Hindi film directed by Shakti Samanta.

I had a fairly good education, studying at all times, during primary and high school, in the best of institutions, the tendency of my parents to measure my performance basis only my academic track record and never to view me on the whole as a capable and intelligent individual, made me rebel. As long as I topped class or came first in school or inter-school competitions and fared better than my neighbours or cousins, I was a 'good boy'. When I slipped, at times and failed to maintain consistent academic performance, I was a 'bad boy'. Though I lacked the maturity then, to understand why I hated being compared to others, or why I believed there was more to Life than academics, my rebellion was confined to merely being anti-convention and anti-establishment. As my rebellious nature started affecting my academic performance adversely, I, in turn, started to hate being called the 'black sheep' of the family – which I was called unfailingly!

In trying to prove that I was worthwhile, and could be successful without being academically proficient, subconsciously, I began to pursue a style of living – personally and professionally – that was built on the twin pillars of seeking fame and fortune. I wanted people to know about me and I wanted to be rich! To be sure, I got what I wanted. As a journalist, I excelled in what I did. Fame, recognition, and what I thought was respect, followed. In my professional employment, I earned more than others my age. I never created assets though but led a Life that was and continues to make an aesthetic statement. I strove to give you both and *Mom* – up until we could afford to – the very best. Never luxury, because I don't see value in it but certainly, high-quality Life experiences. This way of Life got me addicted to emotions that, as I was soon to discover, were ruinous.

As I was able to do things that most people with my background could not achieve normally, I developed an ego. It refused to allow me to listen to others' opinions. I had good hearing, but never listened to what I heard. I have never quite accepted it till now but I guess I was also jealous of others' success and tried to reason to myself that I was the better individual. This gave me the false notion that I was superior – perhaps, even exalted. This pushed me to being avaricious about my success. I wanted to protect what I thought I had created. And I wanted to achieve more – more success, more money, and more fame. As a result, I got sucked into a work-trap that allowed me to justify that I had no time for the family. That my children, you both, have to fend for yourselves, just as I had had to. That being loyal to your wife and being a provider – meaning, meeting your bills – was good enough to be called a caring, loving, family man.

Between *Mom* and me, it was she who had her priorities set as family first and business next. I had business and only business, and only then maybe, family, at times, when it was unavoidable!

Mom was as involved with our business then as she is today. While I managed the business financially and handled client delivery, *Mom* managed business development, the people on our team and our creative function. She came with a better upbringing. She had studied at Rishi Valley,[60] where her parents had taught, and was brought up to believe that quality of Life was determined by being loving and caring; laughing, watching nature, and being compassionate. I loved her and continue to love her for being unchanged despite my influence on her! She often expressed to me that I must not be so driven about material success, that I must make time for you both because you were growing up and would soon set-off on your lives' journeys. I never thought of her as a nagging wife but I didn't see a need to heed her sane counsel.

My professional success had blinded me. My journalistic career and my stints with the corporate sector, for someone with my background, were pretty successful. The Firm, **imag*equity*+®**, that I had founded with *Mom* in 1996 was a niche Reputation Management Consulting Firm, the first from Asia and the only one in India. Our proprietary model, **T*r*M**® (Total Reputation Management) was unique.

---

[60] Rishi Valley – a residential school in Andhra Pradesh, a South Indian state, belonging to the Krishnamurti Foundation, founded by the famous spiritual thinker J. Krishnamurti.

It offered companies consulting services across four verticals: Corporate Strategy, Organizational Behaviour, Marketing, and Communication. The first two built internal experience and the latter built external visibility for an organization. Together, all four built an organization's reputation. We offered all four as a package, in a single Program. We did great business and our clients, their CEOs in particular, acknowledged and celebrated my ability to lead, strategize and deliver unquestionable value on all our mandates. This made me believe even more that we were the best, and invincible. While this level of confidence is important to win – in Life and business – sometimes, as I discovered, it blinds you and prevents you from seeing yourself slip and fall.

We were a small, mom-and-pop shop, a boutique consulting Firm between the years 1996 and 2000. We had three clients. On Sunday, May 21, 2000, *Mom* and I sat at a restaurant table on a cobble-stone pavement in Montmartre[61], in Paris, sipping exquisite French Merlot. A couple of days earlier, we had been in Copenhagen attending a global Reputation Management Conference. We had won an award from the apex body for Reputation Management; the New York-based Reputation Institute, for 'The Best Practitioner

---

[61] Montmartre – a hill in the north of Paris, known for the white-domed Basilica of the *Sacré Cœur* on its summit and as a nightclub district.

Paper' for our **T*r*M**® model at the Conference. We were intoxicated by the wine and the award that evening! It was a big recognition for a small Firm like ours. I asked *Mom*, an all-important question, which would change our lives forever – "Should we continue to be a *mom*-and-*pop* shop or should we grow our reach and business?"

Mom asked me another question in reply, the same question she has always asked me every time we have talked about our Vision for the Firm or the family: "*Dad*, what gives you joy?"

I remember answering, "I want to be known for putting Indian consulting on the global map. I want to leave behind an institution like McKinsey & Co."

That sealed it. We took an Air France flight back to Mumbai, en route to Chennai, later that week. And on the flight, we built our expansion plans, our castles, literally, in the air! Till then, we had not borrowed a penny. We had six people on our team then and still worked out of our home office. We had been billing well while keeping both our client count and our team count low. Our focus on delivering quality and creating value for clients had grown both our reputation and our business.

Now, we planned to change all that. We decided to hire better quality talent and open new offices. Beginning, of course, with moving our family out of the 'office' and giving our Firm a dedicated, refurbished workplace! I have often heard people say that time and events conspire to deliver destiny. So it happened with us too. Client count doubled to six by March 2002 and the team grew to 12 people as well.

In April 2002, a dream client arrived. This was a Hong Kong-based multi-level marketing company, which had a sullied reputation and they wanted it fixed. They had been referred to us by one of our early clients from 1996! This new client wanted us to manage their reputation globally, though at that time they were mainly based out of Asia and the Middle East. Their billings with us were equal to that of our other six clients combined. So, literally, on the day we inked this contract, we had doubled our revenues for the entire fiscal of 2002~2003. This is what ambitious me had been wanting all along. We brought on board three more people to service this new client. And over the next 12 months we transformed this client's culture and reputation dramatically, across seven countries in Asia, making them respected and admired by local communities and their own customers.

So, we were not just hopeful, we were *certain*, of getting an expanded mandate which included the Americas, when our contract came up for renewal in April 2003. We were so close to our Vision of becoming the Indian consulting Firm for the world! We were going to be operating out of the US soon. In preparing to showcase our readiness and willingness to partner with this client and grow with them, we recruited four more people between

January and March 2003 to work exclusively on this relationship.

There were a few rough edges though that needed smoothening for our contract to be extended. We were aware of some key members in the client's leadership team who dissented with their CEO on our role and their company's growing reliance on us. My colleagues who were working on the relationship warned me of a possible hurdle or deal point coming up during the contract extension negotiations, but I did not take them seriously. Because I have always believed – and still do – that people will always have opinions but we must keep moving forward.

At the client's Board meeting, on Friday, April 4, 2003, in Kota Kinabalu, in Sabah, East Malaysia, I made a presentation on what we had achieved on our mandate with them and what we had in mind going forward. I proposed an engagement value of ₹2 Crore ($400,000) annually. The Board, comprising members representing 14 nationalities, gave my presentation a standing ovation. Post my presentation, I was taken into an ante-room where the CEO of the company, a Malaysian-Tamil of Sri Lankan origin, invited me to complete the new engagement discussions and formalities with his COO (Chief Operating Officer) and CFO (Chief Financial Officer).

Leaving the three of us in the room, the CEO departed to join another meeting, saying, "What is being proposed is for you to personally benefit more from our association, AVIS."

The discussion began in right earnest. However, a few minutes into the conversation, the COO put forth a set of documents that I soon discovered, were incorporation papers for a new venture in Hong Kong, which would be carved out of an amalgamation between our companies. I tried to quickly make sense of this surprising development. I was to be the CEO of the new Firm and would have to relocate to Hong Kong. Our Firm would be acquired by the client for ₹60 Lakh ($120,000) and I would get a salary of ₹1 Crore ($200,000) annually. I was, naturally, startled with this turn of events.

I was also upset that I had not even been sounded out on this proposition, which, to me, appeared to be the COO's brainchild. His body language was unfriendly and his communication terse. Besides, he had been one of the principal dissenters on the Board. So I wasn't entirely surprised by his coldness. Nevertheless, business negotiations are sometimes engineered for higher leverage, I thought, as I put forward the following points: 1. Our Firm was not for sale. 2. I disagreed with the valuation they had placed of ₹60 Lakh on our Firm. This amount actually was the value of this client's billing with us in 2002~2003 and I wondered how – and *why* – they had proposed a service contract's value as the Firm's value? 3. I insisted that we continue only with the service contract, fee-based engagement model.

The COO responded, with continued hostility, to my points. All of his sentiments were hurtful but one, in particular, ended the meeting abruptly. He said that he did not see any great value in our Firm and saw only me as a valuable asset. Their company, he said, was basically getting me on board, spending more than 'market value for talent' just so that I accept their proposition.

"And as regards the valuation," the COO continued, "*what more do you think a small, boutique Indian Firm should be worth?*"

I was aghast. I am Indian. And a proud Indian, like millions of others in our country. Our Firm, employing a fine set of young Indians, talented, creative, and passionate, had delivered so much value to this client, and they were making this ridiculous proposal to us and, worse, presenting their offer so pathetically, while demeaning me, my Firm and my country? I looked at the CFO, a Canadian of Polish origin, who had not spoken a word. He had been a great champion of our work on their Board, and I always thought he was objective. However, that day, it appeared, he chose not to be.

He merely said, "AVIS, this proposal has been approved by our Board and is in *your* best interests."

I politely, yet firmly, declined their offer and invited them to rethink their stance. The COO said he instead would want me to rethink.

Then in a sudden display of uncalled for animosity, he said, "*Listen, we can't pay more for an Indian Firm. Take it or leave it!*"

I rose from the meeting table and gathering all my papers, and laptop, started to leave the room. As I was walking out the door, the COO called out, "You don't know what you are walking out on AVIS. Your Firm will suffer!"

I would understand the import of what he said, and why he said so, much later. *But at that moment, I was fighting for, not just my pride and dignity, but my Firm's and my country's too.*

I snapped back, "My Firm is Indian. And it will survive. You will see."

I have often been told that I am too hot-headed. And that I am an emotional fool. I have also been celebrated for my ethical stance and my principled, often unrelenting, stand on doing what's right rather than getting past with what appears to be right. And each time I have reviewed my actions, I have always felt that I would never be at peace doing something wrong, even if it was convenient. That day, when I called *Mom* from Kota Kinabalu, to update her on this bizarre turn of events, I knew, fearfully, what we were going to have to deal with when I returned. This client accounted for 50% of our revenues. With this deal falling through, it appeared with alarming certainty that we would have problems paying salaries and meeting operating expenses for the month of April 2003 and onwards.

That month was also crucial for another reason. We had, in March 2003, hosted a two-city Talk tour for the *Guru* of Reputation Management, Dr. Charles Fombrun, founder of the New York-based Reputation Institute, in India. We had done that as part of our expansion strategy to promote awareness for our business, the industry and our Firm. Bills relating to this event series, held at the Taj Group[62] of Hotels, were due to be paid later in April. As I sat in my Business Class seat on my Malaysia Airlines flight, bound for Chennai, I was angry, upset, hurt, worried, scared and clueless about how we were going to survive this crisis. I was also feeling defeated because the CFO of the client company had told me, in confidence, that one of my own team members, who was managing this relationship alongside me, had disclosed how crucial this client engagement was for us – that we had a 50% revenue exposure to them – to the COO. This information, I surmised, gave the COO confidence, however misplaced, that if pushed to a corner, I would capitulate and sell out!

I was so angry that I had been outwitted for no fault of mine or that of my Firm! We had done great work for this client. We expected an extension of the contract at a higher value. Why, anyone would have expected that! Yet here was the client, disregarding the contract extension completely, wanting 'me' to join them and to achieve that end,

---

[62] Taj Group – India's first and premium hospitality chain.

employing a devious method – of arm-twisting me into selling out! And my own team member had a hand, wilfully or otherwise, in this petty conspiracy? Why? *Why is Life being so unfair?*

I did not realize then that Life never answers our whys. And that Life never promised anyone any fair play.

When I returned to work on Monday, April 7, 2003, I had made two strategic decisions, in consultation with *Mom*, and went ahead with implementing them. 1. We would not rollback our ambition. We were an ethical Firm and we had done nothing wrong. We would march on, boldly. So, we would borrow money from banks and meet the commitments we had to our small pool (then) of creditors and fund the expansion that we had already begun. 2. We would not lay-off any team member and we would encourage the team to put their backs to the wall and help us rebuild the business from the setback we had received.

Ours was a darling team, split evenly between the genders. The average age was 22. All of them wacky, spirited, hard-working, diligent souls. We had built a phenomenal work atmosphere that was known in the job market as a 'great place to earn, learn and lead'. My Executive Assistant then, for instance, who was also working with me on this client relationship, was a young, brilliant, strappy man, Venkatesh Srinivasan, whom you both know as Venky. He had an MBA from IIM-B[63] and had joined us from PepsiCo. Our profit centre heads for new operations in Bengaluru, Pune and Mumbai were smart folks who came from advertising, media and hospitality backgrounds. The 14 people on board then were driven and aggressive. We called them '*mintmakers*'. Our Firm's identity was built on the humble mint leaf. We declared proudly, that just as the humble mint, which never comes to the forefront nor takes centre-stage in any recipe, but repairs, reenergizes, rejuvenates and refreshes the human body when consumed, our Firm too delivered those outcomes to client organizations. Our *mintmakers* were inexperienced but smart and each had a deep desire to change the world. *Mom* and I cared for them like we cared for you both!

On Wednesday, April 9, 2003, I called a team meeting. All our *mintmakers* trooped into my office. I kept the door open and asked all of them to cram up together on one side. I then drew an imaginary line on the ground. I told them of the incidents of Kota Kinabalu and explained, in depth and detail, the consequences of that development. I announced that those who could not handle the uncertain times coming, could cross the imaginary line and leave through the open door. I warned everyone, who would choose to stay back, of salary delays and painful cash crunches till we got the business back on track. We were down by 50% on our

---

[63] IIM-B – Indian Institute of Management, Bengaluru.

revenues and had to bounce back, at least to the same level that we were at in the last fiscal. When I invited people to speak or leave or both, all of them spoke pledging their unconditional support. Just one of them indicated that she wanted to leave. She said that she wanted to speak to me in private. Inviting her to stay back after the meeting was over; I proceeded to thank the *mintmakers* for their support, understanding and willingness to fight back. At the end of my emotional pitch, I broke down and cried inconsolably for several minutes. Each member of the team had moist eyes. We all hugged each other and celebrated a true moment of the team spirit that had come to define the culture of our Firm.

The lady who wanted to speak to me alone stayed on as the others filed out of my office. Fairly succinctly, she said she was resigning to join the same client whose bizarre proposal had put us in this situation. She said, in owning the relationship and servicing the engagement, she had begun to like their work culture and felt that her ambition to be a globe-trotting manager would be better achieved with them than with our Firm. I was quite hurt, but I said nothing. I simply accepted her resignation and after she left the room, as *Mom* looked on, I banged my clenched fist on my desk several times in desperation, in frustration. We had been betrayed. But we would fight back. Our team believed in us.

"We will win!" I told *Mom*. She agreed, hugged me, and kissed me.

That fiscal year – 2003~2004 – the *mintmakers* fought back admirably. Salaries were backlogged by two months, creditors always waited in the front office demanding payments, but we grew our client base. We now had 18 clients. We had 30 team members and operations in six Indian cities. And our revenues were almost the same as the previous year, *without* the client with whom we had separated!

In our rage to prove a point to ourselves, and I take full responsibility for this, we failed to monitor two key indices: 1. Our debt was growing. Touching almost ₹1 Crore ($200,000) at this time. 2. Our profits were wafer thin, ₹4 Lakh ($8000) on a revenue of ₹1 Crore ($200,000).

For a Firm which was essentially into services, this was bizarre. Yet, for us, this was also a grim reality. Since we believed in paying good salaries and working with the best talent the market could offer, our biggest expense was salaries!

What was worse, we didn't discover the mess until April 2004, when we reported impressive top-line figures of ₹1.64 Crore ($360,000) and an appalling profit of ₹1 Lakh ($2000). By then our debt had doubled. *Mom and I slowly realized we had dug ourselves into a deep, dark hole.* We are still trying to extricate ourselves from it!

It was not the debt situation that woke me up. What shocked, startled and jolted me awake was that I was living with abysmally poor quality of thought. I felt I was riding two horses galloping in two different directions! One had me chained to ego, conceit, anger, and my ambition to prove to the world that I was a winner – so I was always combative. The other made me pursue fame, professional brilliance and creative leadership – so I was always on the edge. It all seemed so meaningless, in the midst of daily cash-flow crises. It was like being on a treadmill, running faster and faster, yet, still being in the same place! I had started hating going to work each morning. There was *no* joy in working, in leading our Firm anymore!

I realized that it was time for me to urgently re-examine my Life.

I came to the following conclusions:
1. We had intent and integrity.
2. We were in a great business: Reputation Management Consulting.
3. We were the best in the world: our many clients and the industry's apex body, the New York-based Reputation Institute, would vouch for that.
4. But we were in an ICU[64]-like situation. And we had not discovered it until that moment!

It could not have been more illogical. Why were we in a mess? Why were we struggling?

---

[64] ICU – Intensive Care Unit

This process of inquiry led me to the truth: *I was not thinking right. And hence, I wasn't leading right.* But I just couldn't get started on transforming myself; mainly because I didn't want to accept the truth about myself. I lived in a state of denial for months. The problems stemmed from me but I was angry with the world. I had a tobacco habit. I used to drink every day. I would fly off the handle at all and sundry. At work, people nicknamed me '*chiefscreamer*', punning on my title, '*chiefdreamer*'!

I had been diagnosed with hypertension in 2000 and with diabetes in 2002 but I bulldozed my way through each day – mindlessly, recklessly. By the end of 2003, I had begun hating the face I saw in the mirror each morning. I was *angry* with myself.

By February 2004, our Firm was floundering. There never was any cash to meet our commitments. Outstandings to us from clients were growing. Outstandings to our creditors were growing. I was scared. We were scared.

"*Why me*?" I asked the mirror each morning. "*Why me*?" it answered each time. You could call it neurotic behaviour, but to me, it was real. And so very scary. At night I would wake up sweating, in my air-conditioned bedroom. One night, as you will both recall, I was drunk and drove our dark green Maruti Esteem (a popular model from Maruti Suzuki) into a garbage pick-up truck parked alongside R. K. Salai.[65] Mercifully, I was not injured but the car got a bad dent in the front. I got home finally and spent the night crying in front of *Mom* and you both.

"What was with me? *Why me*?" I asked as I wept. I got no answers. Each of you hugged me. No one admonished. No one lectured. No one dramatized. I am eternally grateful to all of you, *Mom* in particular, to have allowed me the opportunity, dignity, time and space to sort myself out.

On the morning of Wednesday, March 3, 2004, I sat across my diabetologist in Chennai and heard him say, "Son, your blood sugar levels are alarming. I am afraid that you will not live to be 40." I got out of the clinic, barely able to walk in shock. It was Aanch's birthday and I was 37. She had turned 9 that day. I was horrified to think I may not be there to see her grow up, get married, and have a beautiful family! As I reached automatically for my favourite packet of *gutka*[66] (I used to chew up to 20 packets a day and had tried in vain to give the habit up in the past) I paused to think for a moment before I popped the mixture in my mouth. Then, I collected all the packets that I had bought for the day's consumption, walked

---

[65] R. K. Salai – a main thoroughfare in Chennai.
[66] '*Gutka*' – a sachet containing a mixture of betel nut and tobacco, sold widely across India; highly addictive and carcinogenic.

to the nearest garbage bin at the end of the street and trashed all of them. I was not sure I was going to be resolute in my decision to abstain but I was willing to make an attempt. I grudgingly accepted that for my current reality to transform, *I* had to transform.

It was not easy. But *Mom* helped me. We found a dietician named Jyotsana Radja, who we believe is the greatest dietician on the planet, and began a routine that helped me lose 21 kilos in six months. *Mom* lost 17 kilos in the same period. Encouraged, we began a gym/walk routine that we continue even now. In November 2004, my diabetologist took me off medication. My sugar levels are under control, without medication, for over 90 months now, though I am told I will continue to have a diabetic condition all my Life.

Curiously, although I was a compulsive non-vegetarian outside the home, I embraced vegetarianism in July 2004. It was a moral decision and somewhere, deep within me, I felt I was changing. Beginning with thinking differently – about every aspect of my Life. My physical transformation got me to *accept* that a lot can happen with thinking *right* and I began to dig deeper.

My explorations led me to discover that my reality and our Firm's were deeply intertwined with what I was thinking. While we had a Vision to be a global player, our feet were nailed to the ground. I was leading the Firm rather myopically. My thinking centred on these *mantras:*[67]

1.   Do whatever we can to meet our cash-flow needs.

2.   Delight every single client – without reasoning whether a particular relationship or engagement was profitable and meaningful in the first place.

3.   Retain clients irrespective of whether they paid or not.

4.   Commitments made to clients are sacrosanct, even if it means you shoot yourself in the foot to meet that commitment.

Result: we had begun offering our service *ad hoc,* without a clear Reputation Strategy for our clients. Not that we didn't want or know how to offer such a wholesome strategy, but our clients *prima facie* wanted instant gratification and so, we ended up simply providing media relations services, which is a key deliverable in our **TrM**® Program under the Communication vertical. My analysis led me to the realization that we had stopped being a Reputation Management Consulting Firm and had morphed into a public and media relations services company. *It was a shameful moment of discovery.* Way back in August 1996, on the eve of the 50th year of India's Independence, we had

---

[67] *Mantras* – means principles in Sanskrit.

founded ourselves to be the Indian McKinsey, the Indian Consulting Firm for the world. And here we were, about nine years after incorporation – a plain-vanilla, media services and external visibility company.

At the beginning of 2005, *Mom* and I asked ourselves, if we could transform ourselves physically, what about transforming our Firm? Painstakingly, over 12 weekends between January and March 2005, aided by my able and diligent Executive Assistant, Venky, we drew up a Transformation Blueprint for our Firm. This is when I learnt, though belatedly, that right thinking comes from good health. *Had we not lost those extra kilos and cleaned ourselves up from the inside, physically; we would never have reached the state of right thinking.* This was critical, as we were to discover, because we took a very important, purposeful and Life-altering decision: to press '*CTRL+ALT+DEL*' on our tiny Firm. I was following something which Tom Peters, the management *Guru*, had always championed, and which I believed in: 'If you want to change the culture of a company, you must bomb it!'

We pressed 'CTRL+ALT+DEL' to bomb and reboot our Firm. We were working with 38 clients then and had as many people on our rolls. But we had strayed from our Purpose – the reason we had founded **image*equity*+®** in the first place – of making people realize the value of their Reputation. That could happen, we reasoned, only if people knew and understood that Thinking impacts Behaviour, which impacts Performance, which in turn impacts Reputation. For both of us, work which did not conform to our Purpose held no meaning. Which meant work that did not involve changing thinking and thought in organizations was not going to give us any joy. *And why work where there is no joy?* So, we set in motion separations from 38 clients and over 25 team members. Some of them took place peacefully and several of them with strife. Most of them were gone by July 2005. It was excruciatingly painful and scary.

People didn't take to this change kindly. Clients were upset. One of them threatened to demand that we return the investment he had made in our Firm. Several others tried talking me out of my, and from where they saw it – foolish, strategy. The same team members, who had stood with me and *Mom* in 2003, and through the past two years, now revolted and demanded their overdue salaries. An office assistant who was dismissed because he was found trading data with a rival company for cash and who claimed he was doing so because his salary was not coming on time, filed a police complaint against me saying I had cheated him! Three team members, one of whom had won a best performer award in 2004, a Maruti Zen car, left without notice to set up a competing firm of their own. The entire team in the Bengaluru office, a total of seven team members including the office assistant, moved *en masse*, overnight, to a Mumbai-based PR (public relations) firm that wanted to start operations in South India. A few members started a hate email chain calling me names and forwarded it to clients. One belligerent team member, a lady, accused me of cheating and threatened a law suit. This hostility was nerve-racking and gut-wrenching. Finally, my favourite *mintmaker*, Venky, quit too, saying, while he was fine with the strategy to change course, he wanted to explore a different Life and career. I suspect he was not happy with the 'abrupt and cold-blooded' manner in which I was executing the strategy he had helped put together.

In those months, what kept coming back to me was what I remembered Intel Founder Andy Grove saying in an interview, "Leadership in tough conditions is about tough choices. You never walk a mile in one fine, uneventful session. Progress is always slow and one-step-at-a-time. Be aware that the next pebble can sometimes trip you over."

By September 2005, we had completed most of our mandate. We had disengaged with all but five clients and closed down five offices across the country and deferred indefinitely, mercifully, the decision to open an office in Dubai. We had also helped place or placed directly those few team members, who left while understanding and without protest or mess, in various client companies or referred them to friends who ran companies. We were left with two offices, the one in Chennai with four *mintmakers* and two clients and another in Bengaluru, with seven *mintmakers* and three clients. Per a confidential plan that *Mom* and I had worked out, these *mintmakers* and clients too would have to leave our Firm's fold as we entered 2006.

As envisaged in our Transformation Blueprint, we dropped two key delivery verticals – Communication and Marketing services – and integrated the remaining two, Corporate Strategy and Organizational Behaviour, to offer a new delivery model to our clients. The model focused on awakening people in organizations to 1. Spiritual Empowerment, 2. Developing a Servant Attitude (serving their organizations and customers before thinking they deserved more) and 3. Growing Intelligently.

It focussed on transforming the way top management and teams in organizations thought, behaved and performed. Reputation was to be an intended and perceived outcome of our interventions but never an advertised goal!

We had transformed in thought – from being a Reputation Management Firm, to becoming an Organizational Transformation Firm. From being a multi-member team, we eventually shrank to being a mom-and-pop shop. Just *Mom* and me! Both *Mom* and I don't have a qualification in Human Rescources management nor have we done an MBA. But 10 years of working with people and organizations (through our Firm), and drawing learnings from my earlier stint as a business journalist, helped us hone the skills of understanding how people and organizations behaved. Our delivery model changed from being an all-nuts-and-bolts-serviced-here operation to being purely workshop-driven. *Mom* created the content for my workshop sessions, while I delivered them with an *'aha'*-effect on managers –invoking soul, provoking thought and inspiring action. Word got around of the new, improved AVIS and Vaani Team. *The Week*[68] magazine profiled the top 10 motivational speakers in India in March 2006, and I was, as you will both recall, featured in that elite list. It was humbling, and beautiful.

However, business was never consistent. It was slow and sluggish. People knew us as a great Reputation Management Firm but no one wanted to immediately engage us in the realm of Organizational Transformation. When you are entering the tenth year of your existence as a Firm, while others would have called for celebrations, there we were with no clients, no employees and a whole host of past issues, and the heavy burden of debt to deal with. Simply put, we had *no* revenues all through the year 2007 but had bills – huge ones, mostly debt – to pay month-on-month. It was a chaotic period of my Life. Our lives.

---

[68] *The Week* – India's leading newsweekly from the Kerala-based Malayala Manorama Group.

Were we right to embark on the Transformation Blueprint? Was the *'CTRL+ALT+DEL'* strategy the right one? Would we survive? Would the next pebble trip us over? These questions led me to what I call *total surrender*.

I was sure, as was *Mom*, that the new delivery model gave us joy. The few projects we had got in 2006 had made us believe that this was it. We knew that this was our *raison d'être*. We were convinced that awakening managers to the power of thinking right could change the way they led their lives and their organizational mandates. This, in turn, would change the way the organizations performed and profited in the competitive corporate world.

People, who know our story, sometimes tell me that I am courageous. I am not sure if I am but I always set out to do something *only* if I have great conviction in it. The clarity and conviction in my beliefs, in ourselves, in our business model, came from my daily practice of *mouna* which I had begun in mid-2005.

It happened providentially. One day, in November 2004, I had chanced upon this wonderful quote by Swami Vivekananda,[69] *"The World Is Not For Cowards: Do not fly. Look not for success or failure. Join yourself to the perfectly unselfish will and work on. Know that the mind which is born to succeed joins itself to a determined will and perseveres. Live*

---

[69] Swami Vivekananda – a Hindu spiritual thinker who lived and taught between 1863 and 1902.

in the midst of the battle of Life. Anyone can keep calm in a cave or when asleep. Stand in the whirl and madness of action and reach the centre. If you have found the centre, you cannot be moved."

I found Swami Vivekananda's perspective inspiring, challenging! I kept getting provoked by so many issues on a daily basis: a collection delay, an unresponsive, prospective client, a traffic jam, an irate creditor. Anything and everything ticked me off. I yearned for peace and this seemed like an amazing method for achieving peace, if I pulled it off. I was ready and willing to try.

I began my quest to find the centre, my centre. People had talked to me about meditation in the past but I had not found value in their counsel. This time, however, my quest led me to a discourse by the venerable and scholarly Swami Suddhananda[70] on meditation and that helped me make up my mind. However, a few attempts with the practice suggested found me fretting over 'others' disturbing my efforts at being peaceful.

Just when I wanted to give up, I found value in practicing the process laid out in Vijay Eswaran's *In the Sphere of Silence.*[71] Starting one morning in July 2005, I practiced an hour of *mouna* or *Shuba Mouna Yoga* – a period of complete silence – for 21

---

[70] Swami Suddhananda – a spiritual teacher who taught self-realization and self-awareness.

[71] Vijay Eswaran's *'In the Sphere of Silence'* – a book published by RYTHM House.

days. Every day, I awoke at 4 AM and kept utterly silent for an hour. It was not about silencing the environment. It was about silencing myself. The onus was on me. Not on others! I just would not speak during that hour! I felt I was finally able to drop anchor and still my mind. I did not need to chant or think religious thoughts. I often thought about my work though, my goals, my Vision, my dream. I didn't choose any posture in particular. At home, I would just prop myself up with a pillow on my bed. In hotel rooms, I would use the sofa or sit at the desk. All I ensured was that during that hour I was totally silent. The mind fought me initially but I fought back. Remember, the mind, like our body, does not want to be exercised.

Slowly, two things began to happen. 1. I became calmer. Resultantly, I started smiling more. I acknowledged the presence of my security guard in the building (who had been there for many years now) each morning with a pleasant greeting. I started thanking people for small acts of support – my driver, my assistant, the flight attendant, the waiter in a restaurant. 2. I became bolder. Or rather, fear, when faced, delivered courage; which in turn spawned confidence, faith and resilience. The end of the story – that we are winners, who are on this planet to build and lead the Indian McKinsey, became clear to me.

This was fun, I discovered, and I began wanting more. Self-taught in the practice of dropping anchor, and stilling the mind, I experimented with

a technique of peeling away sounds around me and
slowly going into myself – to my centre. What used
to take up to 30 minutes or in times of turmoil even
an hour, started taking just three minutes to attain
– my centre, that is. This is when I could hear every
sound but listened to none. What I listened to was
my inner voice – which too, at most times, was
silent. As I slipped into that silent state, at airports,
in the midst of bustling traffic in my car (I stopped
driving actively in 2004) with the FM radio blaring,
or even in meaningless client meetings where
you are called in as a consultant, (occupational
hazard!), I found myself visualizing **image*quity*+**® as
a global consulting Firm. I saw us getting clients.
Clients who would be serious about building
culture and character in their organizations, and
developing a work ethic that would give them a
strategic competitive advantage, and clients who
would have intent and integrity to embark on a
transformational journey that our new business
model offered. I visualized them compensating
us justly for our time and I visualized successful
completion of all mandates. I visualized better
relationships: with both of you, spending time with
you and being part of your lives; with my parents,
with whom I had been estranged for much of my
Life up until now. I visualized that people would
remember me not as an 'angry, ambitious, foul-
mouthed man in a hurry' as I was often called by
observers, but as a 'calm, friendly, well-mannered,
mature person'. I visualized repaying every penny

that we owed people, with interest, with gratitude and without acrimony.

A couple of years before this transformation happened within me, for reasons purely associated with my position as CEO and Co-Founder of our Firm, I had stuck a little sign on my office door: 'Seek within and ye shall find'. I have no shame in admitting it, but I had done so, because I had then believed in demonstrating I was Mr. Know-It-All, Mr. Right and Mr. Doer. One morning, in December 2006, when I looked at that signage, it came to me in a flash, like lightning. *I had indeed sought within and found my true Self.*

This moment of self-discovery and identifying what gives us joy, helped me deal with business uncertainties. With debt ballooning, clients not signing up, you both growing up and your attendant aspirations having to be funded; in my previous state I would have been completely incapable of leading myself, our precious family or our challenged Firm, (that *Mom* and I regard as our special child!) but now, I was able to do precisely those things and do them well. Even if I was unable to solve a problem on a given day, I was at least able to face it, resolutely and calmly.

Our Firm's operational and financial challenges are too huge to be fixed and overcome in any time frame that we, as mere mortals, can plan for. Between 2007 and 2011, we have led a hand-to-mouth existence. We have barely been able to meet

living expenses for us and for Aash in Chicago
in this time. Business has been unpredictable.
Because we only take up mandates that give us
joy and allow us to create value for our clients we
often go through periods of abject pennilessness,
yet we find ourselves peaceful, happy, in bliss.
There were times, and there continue to be times,
when we do not have cash to buy groceries. We
had to sell a laptop to pay the fees for you Aash,
in your final year at high school in Chennai,
and every single day was spent in pushing back,
pleading with reasonable creditors and embracing
the humiliation and verbal abuse heaped on us
by the more hostile ones. Facing the legal action
initiated against *Mom* and me, and our Firm, and
attending to those matters diligently had become
a part of our schedules. Several friends helped us
in the second half of 2007 and we haven't yet been
able to repay them. All this can take a heavy toll on
you, often making you grieve and feel very guilty.
It did initially and would have entirely consumed
me by now but because we now operate from our
core of joy, doing only what brings us both joy and
profits, we have been able to insulate ourselves
from the problem. The problem remains but our
ability to deal with it has gone up phenomenally!

Mom and I discovered that while we are
financially bankrupt and insolvent, we are
not bankrupt emotionally, professionally,
intellectually, morally, ethically and definitely
not spiritually. Spirituality, I have learned, is the

flowering of inner awareness. It is this awareness that made us realize that our true Purpose is to share the learnings from this phase of our Life and awaken fellow human beings. Money is only incidental. This phase has taught us that chasing money doesn't get you anywhere. However, we understand that it is our duty, and we remain committed, to repay every single rupee we have borrowed from people, with full interest. We will not shirk this responsibility.

To be sure, having made strategic mistakes in 2002 and 2003, and not realizing them until 2004, retooling our business model and bombing and rebooting the Firm in 2005, to struggling to re-establish ourselves and our new way of creating and delivering value over 2006~2010, we have received the desired quality of work and compensation only in the last 12 months, which is in 2011. Our recovery is taking a long time because we refuse to compromise. People have advised us to seek a job, or go into other businesses like enter the flourishing real estate trade or use our high-level corporate contacts to start an executive search and placement firm or even become Amway distributors! We did try to get jobs but were unsuccessful. We also believe that there is no question of doing anything for money. *Whatever we do has to give us joy!*

We created, and practice successfully, a framework for joy-and-profit realization with our business model. The framework operates on the following principles: 1. We take up work only if it gives us joy doing it and allows us to create value for our client. We will quote what we believe is just compensation for our work and value. 2. If the client can afford it, great. If the client can't afford it, but the work will give us joy, we will accept whatever fee the client is willing to give as long as the fee does not fall below a threshold we have fixed. 3. In situations where the client is good, but cannot afford even the base fee, we will still do the work, as long as there is joy and an opportunity to create value, but take whatever fee the client is willing to pay, in the name of our favourite charity, RASA, a Chennai-based NGO[72] (www.rasaindia.org) that educates and empowers special children though music and dance. This framework has ensured that we do what gives us joy. Post 2005, all business, however intermittently, has come only basis this framework. This framework may not have delivered oodles of cash into our bank account but has definitely delivered bliss.

Our bliss brought us to a simple premise which led us to our Core Purpose, our *raison d'être*. I realized that what gives me joy and what defines my core competence best is my ability to invoke soul, provoke thought and inspire action through

---

[72] NGO – Non-Governmental Organization, a non-profit, voluntary body engaged in activity with a charitable, service, participatory or empowering orientation.

my workshops. *Mom* complements me perfectly by preparing the content. We understand that nobody, *nobody*, wakes up to do a bad job. Yet, why doesn't great quality work get done on a daily basis in organizations? *Because people are busy 'earning a living' and not 'living'.* They just exist! So, they need to be inspired to seek spiritual empowerment, to develop an attitude to serve before they say they deserve more and to grow their lives and careers intelligently.

Workshop after workshop, client after client, in the last five years, it has been proven that this model can deliver both joy and profits, for us and our clients and their managers, officers and employees. The money we have earned, however, has been barely enough to help meet our living expenses. There was never enough to repay our debt. When we were not making money, we were still creating value for our clients and for RASA.

While our commitment to our business model was unshakeable, miraculously, we received a cosmic affirmation, a validation of our strategy and our true Core Purpose on Easter Sunday, 2009.

On Saturday, April 11, 2009, I got a call from Philip Sir, a client and dear friend from Kochi, Kerala.[73] Philip Sir had last visited Chennai in January 2008 to look me up when he had come to know of our situation. He had given me ₹1000 ($20) and said, given his own circumstances and

---

[73] Kerala – a South Indian state.

priorities, he couldn't afford to help us more. He requested me to accept the money as his humble *Vishu Kani nettam.*[74] He is a big man, Philip Sir, about 15 years older than I am and in his kind eyes, I saw a graceful energy drench me with a blessing, as I accepted the money. *That money helped us last a week as a family!*

He had also given us a Life-saving engagement by paying for my airfare and inviting me to conduct a day-long workshop with his team at a small processed-foods company in Thrissur, Kerala, in February 2008. He said his company could afford only ₹10,000 ($200) as fee to us but agreed to pay it in cash at the end of the session. We were so cashless that I didn't think. I just grabbed that opportunity. That money, when I brought it back from the trip, helped us buy groceries and last the rest of that month! He was also generous enough to offer me a chauffeur-driven car to visit Guruvayoor[75] and our native family deity in Athipotta[76] in Palakkad district, Kerala, while on that trip. Although I have evolved, thanks to this experience, and do not see great value anymore

---

[74] *'Vishu Kani Nettam'* – a cash offering given by elders to younger members in the family on Malayalam New Year, which normally falls in mid-April; it is seen as a token blessing and is believed to usher in good times.

[75] Guruvayoor – where a famous shrine to Lord Krishna is located, near Thrissur in Kerala.

[76] Athipotta – a small village, 21 kms from Palakkad in Kerala, where AVIS' family deity is enshrined.

in pilgrimages and temple-hopping in times of distress or otherwise; at that time, those visits were important: to believe, to know that a Higher Energy would take care of all that it has created! Of course now, I do know that the Higher Energy resides within us.

Within you. Within me.

For those reasons and others, when Philip Sir called that Easter weekend, I was happy. He said he had been, minutes before calling me, in front of Mother Teresa's tomb, at Mother House, the headquarters of the Missionaries of Charity, in Kolkata. He had been serving as a volunteer at homes run by the Missionaries of Charity, during Lent[77] that year. That Saturday was his last day in Kolkata. He was returning to Kochi transiting via Chennai. He wondered if he could drop in at home for breakfast on Easter Sunday. I told him that he was most welcome!

I picked up Philip Sir from the airport. At home, we had a sumptuous breakfast of hot *idlis*, *sambar*, *coconut chutney* and *molagapodi* with *yennai*.[78] His flight to Kochi was not until later that afternoon. So, we moved into our study. Philip Sir wanted to

---

[77] Lent – a solemn religious observance by Christians, spanning six weeks from Ash Wednesday to Easter Sunday

[78] *Idlis, sambar, coconut chutney* and *molagapodi* with *yennai:* a typical South Indian breakfast of steamed rice cakes, with lentil broth, a coconut sauce and chilli powder with oil for accompaniments.

know how we hoped to fix the business and our lives. I told him that the 14 months since we had met had been a great learning experience. I said my daily practice of *mouna* gave me clarity and we now knew why we had been created on this planet. We now knew what our Core Purpose was.

Philip Sir smiled and asked what that Core Purpose was.

I got up and went to the white board and wrote the following words in blue marker ink: *"To awaken people to the new way of thinking, living, working and winning."*

Even as I explained what the 'new way' was, which is spiritual empowerment, serving, right thinking and growing intelligently through Life, Philip Sir rose from his chair. He took a red marker pen from the holder and walked up to the white board. He placed a big huge 'X', on the word *'new'* and wrote the word *'right'* above it. The statement now read: *"To awaken people to the right way of thinking, living, working and winning."*

As *Mom* and I looked on, obviously perplexed, Philip Sir went on to deliver an impromptu sermon: "When you say 'new way', AVIS, you are saying you invented it. Did you? Of course you did not. Spirituality is as old as mankind. Or older. You are merely sharing a way that you found and which has worked for you. AVIS, be humble. No matter what happens in your Life, stay grounded. You or I or Vaani create nothing. We cause nothing.

Neither our successes nor our failures. We are merely executors of a cosmic will. You have been put through this experience to learn from it and you want to share this 'right way' with others. By all means, do so. You are an amazing speaker. I have heard you. You have the ability to transform how people think. I have experienced it myself. My only wish for you is, no matter how successful you become, never claim any of that success as your own. You are only an instrument."

So saying, he reached into his shirt pocket and pulled up a very small re-sealable zipper storage pouch that had a rose petal in it. The petal had not dried completely and I could see its purple-pink hue as Philip Sir held it up.

He said, "Yesterday, when I said my last prayers at Mother Teresa's tomb and bowed to take her blessings, I was reminded of you suddenly. I don't know why. So when I took a petal for my wife and family, I decided to take one for you and Vaani as well. Here it is. I am not sure I understand what I am doing. I am not sure you understand either. Maybe the reason will manifest much later. For now, accept this petal as a blessing from an apostle of service. May you both overcome your problems and may you too serve humanity, touching lives and making a difference."

Mom and I were in tears as we received the petal. We hugged Philip Sir as he bid us goodbye. I dropped him off at the airport and haven't met him since that Easter Sunday of 2009. The petal still sits on my desk, safe in the tiny re-sealable zipper storage pouch. Both are inside an old plastic film roll can.

What I learnt from him, through him, is now a prayer that I say to myself each time I am leading a workshop: *"I am but an instrument. Whatever the audience must learn today from my experiences, let that learning happen. The message is not mine, the stage is not mine. I am a mere microphone. And no microphone can take credit for the message!"* That my bliss has the blessings of one of the noblest of all creations in the history of humankind – Mother Teresa; overwhelms and sobers me, each time I am in front of an audience.

The important learning here is that *only* when you are thinking right will you encounter the energies which will propel you forward, towards your destiny. I am not saying we have solved all our problems but we know that our destiny is *not* to suffer them endlessly. *Mom* and I know what our Core Purpose is, we know it gives us joy, we know we are following our bliss. Therefore, we know, as Joseph Campbell, the American mythologist and writer, so beautifully said, "When you follow your bliss, doors will open where only walls existed and only you will be able to see those doors."

In completing this wonderful project for this client in Navi Mumbai today, we walked through one more of those doors. This was not a client we knew of, nor did they know us. One of my classmates from school, pinged me on email in March this year, when I was watching the ICC Cricket World Cup 2011[79] on TV at home, and asked if we took up culture-building mandates. I jumped on seeing that email. We were up against a dead end: no cash again, no clients. I replied saying we do. She connected us on email to the CEO of this company whom she knew because he used to be her husband's boss at a large multinational paints company. *Can you believe it? Someone from school, with whom you had lost contact for 30 years and simply reconnected on Facebook, connects you to someone who ends up giving you a career-defining mandate!*

This too is Life, my dear Aash and Aanch and this kind of Life happens *only* when you follow your bliss. Bliss has been wrongly promoted as something you attain. It is something that you are. To each one of us it is different. Which is why Campbell says, follow *your* bliss. Knowing what it is for you, is enlightenment. Now, there is no method to discovering your bliss. Life will take you through many experiences, some amazing, some terrible. You will want to re-live again and again those experiences you love. The common thread that connects the experiences you want to re-live

---

[79] ICC World Cup 2011 – a cricket tournament in the One Day International format that is held once every four years, equivalent of the FIFA World Cup.

are the ones that define your bliss. This is what we have learnt. This is what we have lived through.

I am often asked – if I was not stupid as a business leader, to use borrowed funds to attempt a business expansion? Was I not stubborn to have not accepted the client's offer to buy my Firm and place me and pay me well in Hong Kong? Was I also not emotional when I took that decision to not lay off people who were on our rolls when that client separation happened in April 2003? Wasn't it suicidal to bomb the business in 2005 whereas a more prudent approach would have been to transform in phases? I don't have elaborate answers, because my actions were so simple. I did what I thought was right. If growing a business on debt is a mistake, I have indeed learnt my lesson. If believing in team members, and counting on their support, was a mistake, then I am guilty of it. If I made a mistake in not placing my own personal gain above my country's and my Firm's dignity, then yet again, I plead guilty. And if bombing the Firm was a mistake, in order to do only what gives us joy, then, I own that mistake too!

I am not sure I would have done anything else. Or any better. Maybe a few tactical steps here and there may have been executed differently but the whole approach to retooling our business happened accidentally, and not out of any great strategic design. One thing led to another. Each step led to more and more inner peace. Perhaps the final outcome, the bliss we feel, was part of a larger cosmic design, just as everything else is. Though a lot of our worldly responsibilities, like our debt, remain, I have learnt in these years that the greatest wealth is to be able to do what you love and love what you do. This wealth, you will agree, *Mom* and I have in abundance!

What happened with us may appear unique but it may not really be! Life deals with each person differently, yet the learnings remain the same. I want you both to know that at various times in our lives, we feel lost, to the point of losing ourselves; only so that we can find or rediscover, our true Self, our potential to love, our faith and our ability to follow our bliss!

Any journey, any pursuit, will have its share of challenging times. Often these journeys will be excruciatingly painful. They will drive you to the point of complete despondency and lack of self-belief. You will wonder if you have indeed lost the game of Life. That's when you must take a deep breath and remember that *you* are not playing this game, Life is. Your role is to follow your bliss, to do what gives you joy and happiness. If the pursuit of your dream, your mission or goal gives you joy, despite all the attendant pain, you *must* continue to do what you set out to do.

You can give up if you are in control but how do you give up something that you no longer control, once it has been set into motion? Your role as a voyager is to set out on the journey, which you have indeed. Life's job is to take you to the shore and Life will eventually get you there but not before tossing and turning you around and churning your insides several times over, in the process!

Believe me, everyone has the ability to follow their bliss. Because, doing what you love doing is simple. *We* make it complicated by putting a price tag on it. Life cannot be confined to business models and debt-equity ratios. The top-line and bottom-line, both, in Life is bliss. Follow it. Live it. You will profit from it.

With Prayers For Your Bliss!
Dad

11

Rise In Love

"It is not a lack of love, but a lack of friendship that makes unhappy marriages."

~ Friedrich Nietzsche, German Philosopher and Poet (1844 ~ 1900)

Wednesday, February 10, 2010
9.30 PM: Chennai

Dear Aash and Aanch,

Today, in a courtroom, in the Metropolitan Magistrates' Court premises in Saidapet,[80] Chennai, I met the same woman I had once proposed to, on a half-moon night, under a starlit sky. I could see the same love for me in her beautiful eyes even after all these years.

That woman is your *Mom*!

I had proposed to your *Mom* on Monday, February 22, 1988, under a huge rain tree. Your *Mom* was wearing a white *sari* with colourful floral prints and a white blouse to match. Her hair was tied in a cute ponytail and we were returning from a post-graduate evening college programme we had both enrolled in.

I was 20 then. She was almost 22. We were very close to her home. From the gate of the premises where her family then lived, we had to walk a short distance of about 300 metres to reach their door. The rain tree stood between the gate and their door on a large, well-landscaped ground. I had made up my mind to tell her that it was time we moved our relationship forward. Yet I had no idea about what I was going to say or how I was

---

[80] Saidapet – a middle-class commercial and residential area in south Chennai.

going to say it. I was too young and too uninitiated to even consider kneeling down on one knee and a making a classic, formal (though I am not sure if it can be called romantic) proposal. But I knew that this girl was the one I wanted to be with for the rest of my Life, the one who would be mother to my children and who would love me many years later, in the way she loved me now.

I had met your *Mom* for the first time, only a few months earlier, in October 1987. The following month, just after my 20th birthday, when she sang, *'Tere mere milan ki ye raena...'*, a classic song, from the Amitabh Bachchan-Jaya Bhaduri-starrer *Abhimaan*[81] at our evening college's cultural programme, she took my heart, breath and soul away! She had worn the same white sari on stage that evening too. I was with a gaggle of   girls (!) from my class in the last row of the auditorium, booing all the performers that evening, as college kids are wont to do. But when your *Mom* started to sing, something happened within me. I was both mesmerized and instantaneously drawn to her. Indeed the song she sang is soulful and stirs something deep within the listener. Kishore Kumar and Lata Mangeshkar had sung it with admirable simplicity and an unforgettable, soothing melancholy. Besides, it featured my idol, Amitabh Bachchan, and Jaya, whom he later married. There was an inspiring

---

[81] *Abhimaan* – meaning 'Pride', a 1973 Hindi film directed by Hrishikesh Mukherjee.

romance in their screen personas, and particularly
in this song, which I had connected with when I
first watched the movie. The song would tug at
my heartstrings, each time I heard it, and prompt
me to visualize a future that was so beautiful, so
complete, with my own dear companion for Life!
Maybe those were the reasons why I turned away
from my riotous, even if interesting, friends and got
up to move toward one of the rows in front. As your
Mom continued to sing, with her co-performer and
our classmate Murali, my heart was filled with a
hitherto unknown feeling, a warmth, a longing. You
could call it love! Your *Mom's* beautiful voice, I later
concluded, was why I was drawn away from the
girls in my class towards the only girl I wanted to
know in the whole world. I guess I realized I was in
love – then and there!

It took over four months of knowing her,
her family and for her to understand me and
appreciate me, and my rather strange family –
though I had ensured that *Mom* or *Mom's* family
did *not* meet mine until much later – for me to be
prepared to propose.

But that night I was ready. I was sure it had
to be done. With each step we took that night, I
calculated how much closer we were getting to
their front door. From their living room, I knew an
anxious Padma[82] *paati* would be watching, as she

---

[82] Padma – is the name of Vaani's mother who passed away
in 2001.

always did, her eyes sweeping the large ground and trying to look past the rain tree and the darkness it held under its huge canopy, to the lone streetlight by the gate, to see if we had arrived. It was 9 PM already and we were late, having taken a public transport bus from our college. When we reached the rain tree, and had just about passed it, but were still under its dark canopy, I spoke. Our faces were lit faintly by the moonlight filtering through an opening amongst the branches above us as I turned to *Mom*.

I looked into her beautiful eyes and said, "Aren't we getting dangerously close to each other?"

She stopped in her tracks. She looked into my eyes too. I could see that her eyes had started welling up.

She cried and with all her love, confessed, "Yes!"

It is a 'yes' that I can still hear, whenever I recollect that moment under the rain tree. Neither of us said anything more that night. After a brief, pregnant pause, in which I drew your *Mom* closer to me and held her gaze with mine, we both, with unprepared yet amazing synchronization, started to walk towards the light emanating from the porch of *Mom's* home. I am glad we didn't try to stretch out that conversation because what remains in my memory is what your *Mom* did say, with her eyes, without saying another word! She promised me a lifetime of happiness, companionship, friendship, loving and staying true. That look in her eyes is something I carry with me every day, each moment of my Life.

This morning, at the IXth Metropolitan Magistrate Court in Saidapet, I saw that look in your *Mom's* eyes, one more time. We were in court for a hearing in a case filed by a bank from which we had borrowed money in *Mom's* name. Today is our 21st wedding anniversary. After answering the many calls and messages wishing us, and also after getting a beautiful card from both of you, which Aanch gave us complete with a memorable hug and kiss, we got ready and arrived at the court 10 minutes ahead of the time our case was slated to be heard. The balcony of the courtroom where we had to wait to be summoned – faces the East. The sun was beating down mercilessly on all of us who thronged the balcony this morning.

There were pickpockets and petty criminals, with underpaid and overworked cops keeping them in check. Sweaty lawyers, in their flowing back gowns or in their black coats, went about their business, preparing for the day's hearings for their clients, with a cultivated sense of urgency. There were also some very poor people who looked fearful having been summoned to a court. Court officials walked purposelessly, though feigning busyness, in and out of the courtroom, discourteous to most people, until, of course, someone squeezed a 50 rupee note (about $1) into their welcoming palms while completing an orchestrated handshake. A few people looked like *Mom* and me. Completely out of place. Unintentional 'criminals'. Victims of circumstance. Yet boldly facing Life in the now. Living it for what it is.

As *Mom* looked into the courtroom expectantly, hoping to see the lady magistrate arrive and take her seat on the raised podium, my heart leapt in a rush of romance. I would have kissed your *Mom* had it not been for the courtroom and all these people. I could also feel, somewhere deep within, a huge pang of guilt pierce me. *Was this the way to celebrate a wedding anniversary? Haven't I let your Mom down, landing her in a courtroom, with the status of an accused in a criminal case under Section 138 of the Indian Negotiable Instruments Act?*[83] I always felt I had failed completely as a business leader, but this morning, I felt I had also failed as husband, as a provider, as a protector and as your *Mom's* best friend. My guilt morphed into grief without me even realizing it. I started to fight my tears. I reached out to *Mom*, tapping her on her shoulder. She turned and looked up at me.

And I said, pretty much with no preparation just as I had spoken on that half-moon night, also in February, 22 years ago, "*Mom*, I am sorry. I am so sorry. I am sorry for making our wedding anniversary feel like this. I hope you will forgive me."

---

[83] Section 138 of the Indian Negotiable Instrument Act, 1881, amended in 1988 – a law that deals with the dishonour of cheques for non-availability or insufficiency of funds.

Your *Mom* smiled reassuringly. She seemed not to have even an iota of worry, fear, doubt, guilt or remorse in her.

She replied, *"Pappa,*[84] we have walked to many places together, through so many different times. This is yet another place. I don't care if I am walking to the Malai Mandir in R. K. Puram, New Delhi,[85] or I am in a courtroom or in a suite at the Ritz Carlton Millennia, Singapore, or on top of the Eiffel Tower in Paris or at Tiger Hill, Darjeeling[86], freezing and waiting for the sun to rise! *I am just happy being with you, wherever I am."*

I held her hands tightly in mine, squeezed them, turned away, went to the court's balcony's stone railing, faced the blazing sun and wiped away my tears as they flowed down my cheeks.

As you know, I am younger than *Mom.* So, I have always looked up to *Mom* and her unstated leadership. Yes, I am the more visible decision-maker at home. It was my ambition, unstructured

---

[84] *Pappa* – an affectionate pet name in Hindi for 'Dad'.
[85] Malai Mandir in R. K. Puram, New Delhi – a South Indian temple dedicated to the South Indian God, Lord Muruga, in a New Delhi suburb; Vaani and AVIS had walked 18 kms to the shrine from Vaani's parents' place in New Delhi (they had moved from Chennai to Delhi at that time) in 1988 to fulfil a vow they had made should both sets of parents agree to their marriage.
[86] Tiger Hill, Darjeeling – in the Indian state of West Bengal that offers panoramic views of Mount Everest and Kangchenjunga

and unfettered, that led to our Firm's collapse, and eventually, to our family's insolvency. It was always also my call to quit jobs, take new ones, hire team members, sack them, decide on borrowings or expenditures. Yet *Mom's* leadership of the other part of our Life, the family, the two of you, our health and our peace, has ensured that we have had the nourishing, warm environment at home, that we so badly needed to survive while a storm raged in our external world, often threatening to ravage our hearth and home!

Mom has invested every waking hour of hers in her role as a mother, in both of you – feeding you, bathing you, teaching you and being there for you. I deeply admire her ability to love all of us, her ownership of our family and her sincerity. She has played another role too, admirably – that of my best friend. She would unfailingly stay awake when I came home late, several nights a week at times, drunk, under the pretext of entertaining business associates. She would heat up food and insist I had a warm meal before I went to bed. Even so, she would hold a mirror up to me, talking about my deviant behaviour, without ever affecting my self-esteem.

I remember once in 1994, when we were living in Bengaluru, and she was pregnant with Aanch in her seventh month; I came home inebriated. As she opened the door of our Malleswaram apartment, I threw up on her! Right into our living room! She patiently cleaned up, asking me to take it easy. Whether it was that night, or any other time, whether it was my inability to hold my drink in the early years of our marriage or my ruinous habit of chewing tobacco later, she never nagged or preached.

Yet, *Mom* has never been a doormat or the typical suffering wife of an Indian home. She always said whatever she wanted to in an awakening, encouraging sort of way, inviting me to be responsible, to 'wake up and smell the coffee'. Each time she has done that she has invoked a higher sense of maturity and responsibility in me. I am often asked by friends, observers, family members, as to whether *Mom* has ever protested in all these years that we have spent struggling to just keep our heads above water, through this bankruptcy. The answer is, truly, she has never done so. People who hear this say I am blessed. Or some say I am lucky. I don't know what it means to not have a spouse who understands you, because mercifully I have not had to face such a situation. Knowing and loving your *Mom*, and learning from her, is to continuously rise in love.

I want you both to understand the essence of companionship in Life, drawing upon how inspired I am by your *Mom*. Sooner than you both believe, you too will be in love. You too will meet and want to be with someone whom you want to spend the rest of your Life with. But remember, being in a relationship alone does not mean being in love. Being drawn to someone for their physical attributes is not being in love either. Being happy in someone's presence is also not being in love completely. You are in love completely when you can be someone's best friend and can have that best friend's friendship forever. A best friend is a soul-mate. Someone who can help you see who you are, accept you for what you are and in the future may become one who does not shy away from speaking the truth; holding a mirror and critiquing – not criticising – your actions and someone who is willing to walk with you to where neither of you has been before. A soul-mate is *always* understanding, demanding, forgiving, compassionate, teaching and uplifting.

It is not difficult or too complex to be a soul-mate. You can be one too. Being a soul-mate requires one to know, understand and appreciate the meaning of Life. Life in your teens and early adulthood will be full of exploration. Especially of your sexuality. This is where you will find joy in kissing, feeling and, perhaps, in today's generation, having sex. Please know that there's nothing wrong with any of that. When you get past the physical dimension of love, you begin to see the value of wanting to spend a lifetime with that person. It's a great feeling, full of anticipation. Of your own home, of your own children, of your own Life together; living, happily ever after.

Now, almost everyone who falls in love first and then marries gets into that relationship with the same sentiments and expectations. Then, have you wondered, why do people break up? Why do marriages fail? It is because, relationships, as I have learned from Osho, the Master, signify the death of the same something, that precious feeling that inspired you, in the first place, called love. You love someone when you relate to that person. People fall out of love because in a marriage, while there is a law, a label, society, family, caste and religion – there is no more relating!

I think what has worked for *Mom* and me is that we continue to relate to each other. Age, place, or circumstance, don't seem to affect or pollute our precious, pristine shared space, where our love for each other continues to thrive. It is not something unique to us. We have just made our friendship, our way of relating to each other special. We always say what we think to each other, often disagree animatedly, agree to disagree, and yet never say, 'I told you so'. I remember several times when *Mom* would sit me down and plead with me to put away savings for both of you, for your higher education. I would say, while I agreed with her, that the Firm needed all our money and so, I redeployed whatever cash we accrued in the business. Then we went bust, and ended up being cashless. Every single time we were unable to wire money to Aash's University or buy Aanch anything she needed, or pay for her passage to participate in the exclusive Global Youth Leadership Conference due to be held in Washington D.C., and New York City, in May this year (Aash, you will recall that we were also unable to send you to the US for the same Conference in 2008), despite her having been nominated by her school, I have grieved. But your *Mom* has never ever held me guilty or responsible!

When you fall in love, there are chances of falling out! Yet your *Mom* and I, interestingly, continue to rise in love!

Please know that even 'close' relationships, like your *Mom's* and mine, need a rising in love, a continuous relating, for them to thrive. We are happy we understand this and wish for you to know this too. If the people involved do not connect, relationships wither away like plants do, without water and sunlight. We are not talking about acquaintances that we 'can't get along with' for professional or other reasons, but the people who 'were so close once upon a time, but are no longer'! This is to explain why we grow distant from childhood friends, from spouses whom we dated, romanced and loved deeply once upon a time or siblings that we grew up with. The distances that spring up between us and such people are not because of a lack of mutual respect or admiration but because we have stopped relating with each other. Relating encompasses nurturing, providing adequate sunshine and water, through talking, critiquing, supporting, challenging, caring and sometimes, just being available. Relating means loving someone all the time – irrespective of time, space, behaviour, responses or circumstances.

Remember, Life will change; the circumstances of your attraction will change once you start living with someone. Those circumstances will change again when you get used to living with that someone. There will be more change with age, opportunities, money, challenges, setbacks, death and so many other things. Rising in love means you remain unchanged in your loving of that person, no matter what. Instead of bringing law or definitions and labels or money into relationships, focus on a never-ending relating instead. Love each person in your Life, keep on relating to the other – lover, friend, parent, colleague, sibling, whoever – without pausing to evaluate, analyze or justify. Through the energies of your continuous celebration, the loving, the relating, will enrich both your souls – exponentially, infinitely.

Grateful To Have Learned To Rise In Love!
Dad

12

Wear Your Life On Your Sleeve!

"If you tell the truth, you don't have to remember anything."

~ Mark Twain, American Author
and Humourist (1835~1910)

Saturday, July 11, 2009
4.00 AM: Chennai

Dear Aash and Aanch,

L ate last night, around 10 PM, the cops from
the neighbourhood E4 Police Station[87] picked
me up from home. Accompanying the Sub-
Inspector who came to fetch me, was a good friend
of mine, called Girish Reddy,[88] from whom I had
borrowed money.

When I peered through the peep hole, wondering
who it was at that unusual hour, I saw at first only
the Sub-Inspector (SI) standing outside. When I
opened the door, I saw Girish in the foyer too.
While I was startled, it quickly started to make
sense to me. Girish had made a complaint to the
cops. It would be a matter under Section 420
of the Indian Penal Code (IPC) which deals with
cheating and dishonesty, and is often a matter
that is rabidly contested: the accused will always
claim there never was any intent to cheat while
the complainant will vociferously insist otherwise.
And the idea, of picking up someone late at night
on a Friday for 'questioning' would be obviously to
slap charges that would allow an arrest at the local

---

[87] E4 Police Station – a police station covering the R. A.
Puram and Alwarpet neighbourhoods where AVIS' family
lived.
[88] Real name not disclosed to protect identity.

police station's jurisdiction and discretion, keep the person in police custody over the weekend, while the courts are closed, and deny the person the opportunity to be granted bail instantly. It's a plot that unfolds each weekend across India, unfailingly, often claiming victims like us, who are not hardened criminals but simply trapped in a vicious design of circumstance. Normally, most people would not want to spend a weekend in police custody, hence they would 'settle' matters with the complainant and 'pay' the cops goodwill money to broker a compromise resolution.

Even as all this was dawning on me, the SI spoke when I looked at him, enquiringly, and at Girish, knowingly.

"Sir, Mr. Anand Viswanathan?" the SI asked, and upon getting an affirmation from me, he continued, "This gentleman has made a complaint against you that you have cheated him of some money. I need you to come with me to our Police Station for enquiries."

He was trying to be firm and menacing, with his big whiskers and his uniform. Despite the desperation taking root in me, I noticed the *kumkumam*[89] smeared carelessly on his forehead, perhaps applied at a temple, which he must have visited earlier in the evening.

---

[89] *Kumkumam* – a vermilion-coloured powder, sacred to believers, and applied on the forehead to profess and exhibit faith.

Mom had joined me at the door by then. She too gathered in a jiffy what it was all about. Out of the corner of my eye, even as I looked at *Mom*, I saw Aanch peep out of her bedroom, from where she could view a part of the living room where we were standing, though she couldn't see the officer in uniform at the doorway.

'Who is it Dad?" enquired Aanch.

I replied urgently, ordering her with an unusual tone of authority, "Nothing Aanch. Go into your room!"

I was relieved when Aanch slipped back into her room and closed the door. I looked at Venks *thatha's* room to see if he too was going to come out having heard the doorbell ring. I tried to look for signs of him turning on the lights. He normally went to bed at 9 PM each night and he had done so yesterday as well. He always slept soundly. I was relieved as I could not detect activity in his room.

Aash, you are in India from Chicago for the summer and you had just, about a few minutes before the doorbell rang, gone to your room upstairs to watch a movie on DVD. I felt relieved that you were not watching the movie on the TV in our living room. Or else, *you* would have opened the door for the cop!

I counted our blessings at this moment. 'It is best Aash, Aanch and *thatha* don't know what's going on,' I thought to myself.

Looking at *Mom* I said, "We need to face this too. Let's see where this takes us!"

Mom replied, "Wherever you are going, I am coming with you, *Dad*!" I didn't protest. I knew I will need *Mom* by my side to last the night of 'questioning' and beyond!

I turned around and looked at the SI who was still at the door. Girish stood behind him trying to battle two expressions: he wanted to look tough to justify that he had been driven to taking this step but he couldn't conceal his sheepish look because this is not something friends do to friends. Definitely not in India, where we all know that inviting cops to the party does not mean reaching a resolution. It means getting embroiled in a quagmire of procedures that can be untangled only by both parties usually 'paying up'!

I asked the SI, "Sir, do I have time to change and call my lawyer or are you here to take me away in my night clothes?"

"No Sir, we will wait here. Please change and come," he replied, after looking at the boxers and the white half-sleeved muscle tee I was wearing, rather intently.

I invited him and Girish into our living room and said that *Mom* makes good coffee. I suggested that they enjoy our hospitality while I changed, called our lawyer, Uncle Vijayaraghavan, and came back. He declined the offer, saying he preferred to wait at the door. He appeared to be both officious and ethical, suspecting perhaps that the offer of coffee was a step by me to ingratiate myself. I let him think so.

Mom and I closed our bedroom door and looked at each other anxiously. We didn't speak for a few seconds. We know this kind of stuff happens in India and have seen it in movies or have read of it in the papers: people using political influence to get the police to take or threaten action against people with whom they may have failed business, money or property dealings. The cops, technically, at least in our matter with Girish, do not have the right to intervene in civil matters. I had borrowed money from Girish. I had failed to fulfil the obligation to repay him on time. At best Girish can file a civil suit in a court or deposit any cheque I may have given him for security purposes, and should the cheque bounce, after serving legal notices on me, he can approach the relevant court and file a complaint. The court then issues a summons and if I appear, there is no arrest made in courts in Tamil Nadu. If I don't appear, I am liable to be arrested after the issuance of a warrant. In such a case, I can seek bail after appearing in court. So, there really is no ground for a cop to arrive at anyone's door past 10 PM on a Friday night. Besides, cops in India are overworked, investigating murders and other heinous crimes, providing security to government officials and ministers, and maintaining law and order, even while ensuring sanity on the roads! There are far fewer cops in each police station in

India than there should be and they get pulled in a zillion different directions on a daily basis. The last thing on their minds would be to get involved in a civil, cash loan, matter.

But I have heard that cops love such opportunities. I am told that they love them because they know these are opportunities to milk victims and offenders alike for money. They are aware that normal citizens fear the corrupt police. They know that we know that landing in a police matter means a mess. Simply put, no other language works with most of them than the language of money! *And we don't have money!*

Arresting this flow of thought, I finally spoke. I said to *Mom*, "Put my laptop into my bag. I will call Vijayaraghavan. You change. And let's go."

She replied, "Don't worry about the kids. We will tiptoe out, lock the door. And they will think we are asleep."

I called Uncle Vijayaraghavan. He patiently heard me out. He said that the cops can't hold me in custody without being answerable themselves. Even if they did slap charges under some Sections of the IPC, we can move court on Monday and deal with the matter. He advised me to tell the cops the truth, to demonstrate intent to repay and told me not to sign any documents without his permission.

It was a reassuring call but the apprehension of getting into a hitherto unknown situation was gnawing at me as I changed quickly. In about five minutes we were back at the front door. I asked the SI if I could travel in our car or if he preferred to escort me in his jeep. He said he trusted me to behave myself and said I could indeed drive there in our car.

When we came to the parking lot, we saw two police vehicles, with their red and blue beacons swirling, mercifully without their sirens wailing, and a third, Girish's, in our driveway. They filed out one after the other and we drove behind them. The E4 Police Station is not very far from where we live here in Bishop Garden. As we drove, I told *Mom* that Girish and I had met just a couple of days ago. Girish is a software engineer who works in California. He had given us this money three years ago as a personal loan and we had agreed to pay him four percent interest per month. Prior to this loan, we had borrowed a smaller sum and had repaid it fully with the interest due. Girish, at our meeting earlier in the week, had shared how his brother had suddenly died in an accident and how he was in dire need of the money. I had been writing to each creditor monthly, including Girish, all through 2008 and now, through 2009, explaining the reasons for the delay, and seeking their understanding and patience. The communication was proactive. Few of our friends responded to these emails from me. Girish was one of them. Over the last couple of months, in particular, Girish had been writing to me saying he needed the money back.

These are times when there is not enough money at home to last even an entire month. When our own living expenses are not covered fully, I have not seen any possibility or opportunity to repay anyone, and that includes Girish.

As I drove into CPR Road, having driven through Greenways, Chamiers and reaching the Kaliappa Hospital traffic intersection,[90] *Mom's* phone rang. It was you Aash. Aanch had not gone to sleep. She had called you, Aash, on your mobile phone from the landline in her bedroom, and told you that she found it weird that *Mom* and I should first order her back into her room, then, change in a rush, and leave the house. Aash, you demanded to know from *Mom* what was going on. Honestly children, this is not something that we are going to hide from you forever but neither of you can help us here. This is not information which will help you in any way either. You both will only worry and fear. This will take you away from enjoying the protected environment that we have maintained for you both, untouched by our bankruptcy.

Mom, with this wisdom, replied, *"Dad's* got a headache. We are out to get some pills from the 24-hour pharmacy at Kaliappa Hospital and then

---

[90] Greenways, Chamiers and reaching the Kaliappa Hospital traffic intersection – avenues in the neighbourhood of Bishop Garden, where Vaani and AVIS lived at that time.

grab some coffee at the Park Sheraton Hotel[91]. We should be back in an hour."

I am grateful Aash that you trusted *Mom*, though what she said was not factual, because we didn't want you both worrying and having a sleepless night.

Even as *Mom* was finishing her call with you Aash, we reached the E4 Police Station. The convoy leading us had already parked outside the station. I parked too. *Mom* and I entered the building, with the laptop backpack in tow. The SI waved us towards his small office which had nothing but an arrangement of a few worn out wooden tables and a few benches to sit on, a couple of cupboards that were locked with oversized padlocks and two pedestal fans that were placed diagonally opposite each other. The SI turned one of them on and it went to work noisily.

The SI looked at *Mom* and said, "Madam, I can't have a lady inside a police station after 5.30 PM. We need to question your husband. So, I request you to leave."

I found, just as *Mom* did, the idea preposterous. However constitutional the SI's perspective was and however, unusually, ethical his stance to follow the rulebook was, it appeared to me that a lady was possibly safer inside the premises than

---

[91] Park Sheraton Hotel – a five-star hotel run by the ITC Group in the neighbourhood of where AVIS' family lived

on the dark, deserted, poorly-lit street outside. But there was a certain natural authority in the SI's directive and so, neither *Mom* nor I protested. As Mom prepared to leave, I thrust my wristwatch and mobile phone into her hand. In India, according to stories I had heard, cops can take away these things while making an arrest and then do not return them. They don't always do such things but right now we couldn't afford to lose either of those gadgets because we did not have money to replace them!

I watched; my heart beating fast, helplessly and curiously, as *Mom* walked away from me and then out of the Police Station. From where I was, I would not be able to see her waiting outside.

The SI asked me to sit on a wooden bench and asked Girish to sit in a chair. It was only then that I noticed Girish had brought someone along. This man looked to me to be every bit a villain from a Tamil film. He was big, hairy and burly and wearing a white *khadi*[92] shirt. He had a big moustache, twirled up like some of the people who come from down South, beyond Madurai, in Tamil Nadu. He had a thick gold chain on his neck and wore gold and diamond rings on four fingers on either hand. His *veshti*[93] was spotless and was surprisingly fresh, just as his shirt was, for this late hour. Girish

---

[92] '*Khadi*' – a fabric made from hand-spun cotton.
[93] '*Veshti*' – a white garment that is worn around the waist like a *sarong.*

sat on a chair, wearing a simple pink cotton shirt, a pair of faded blue jeans and slippers.

Girish's companion spoke up. He looked at the SI and dictated, like a client would insist to an inefficient service provider, "I want this man to give my friend Girish the money back now. Or I want you to lock him up. There will be no discussions."

The SI looked at me, and raising his eyebrows twice, in quick succession, indicated to me that he wanted me to comply.

I began speaking softly, in English. Looking first at Girish, I said, "I am sorry Girish for not being able to return your money." Then looking at the SI, I said, "Sir, I have no money. I am bankrupt. I barely make enough for my family to survive. I have paid four per cent interest to this gentleman and closed one loan. Even on this account, I have paid substantial amounts as interest. In the last several months I have paid nothing because I have nothing to pay..."

I would have finished my sentence, but the SI interrupted me impatiently.

He declared, trying his best to sound menacing and trying to convince me of his ruthlessness, "You look decent Mr. Viswanathan. You live in Bishop Garden, one of the poshest areas of Chennai and you want me to believe you are bankrupt? Let me tell you Sir, I have no interest in this matter except ensuring that justice is done to the complainant's claim. I have my night rounds to complete. I will be gone for an hour. When I come back you and Girish need to have agreed upon an amicable payment plan. If you don't, please know that I am a *pollathavan*.[94] I will be ruthless. I have enough authority and know enough law to keep you locked up here this weekend and book you under a non-bailable Section of the IPC. Please get your priorities straight Sir. *Settle. Or suffer!*"

I was not given any opportunity to explain. The SI rose from his seat and gesturing to Girish's friend to follow him, he walked out. Only Girish and I sat in the sparsely-lit office. Behind where the SI had been sitting was an equally dimly-lit, and dusty, cell. What they call a lock-up in India. It had some cardboard cartons with many files in them stacked one on top of another. It had cobwebs on the iron bars of the gate that opened into the cell. I briefly thought whether I would have to spend the weekend there. I wondered what the condition of the toilet here would be like and felt nauseated instantly. But something in me told me to be bold. *I reasoned to myself that if it came to that, I had to endure this experience.* I was very clear, stoic and resolute, about three things: 1. We did not have money to settle with Girish, so we were going to have to face the consequences even as we let Uncle Vijayaraghavan take remedial steps on Monday to quash any charges that may be brought against me tonight. 2. We were not going

---

[94] *'Pollathavan'* – means ruthless in Tamil.

to bribe the cops to get out of this mess. Either I convince the cops that there are no grounds for their actions or I prepare to face the situation. In any case, there was no money for a bribe. And I am eternally grateful for that because it ensured that I could not take the easy way out of the situation. 3. I would face the impending issue of the lock-up with a smile and not resist it. *After all, what was the point in being ready to face Life but not being willing when it came calling?*

I looked at Girish. His face was blank. He was still struggling, I believed, between having failed a friend and having to protect his interests. I decided to help him out.

I said, "Girish, if it helps you recover your money, please persist with your course of action. I told you at our last meeting earlier this week that there was no way I am going to be able to pay you in the next six months at least. And I am not hurt by your actions. You will continue to remain a good friend who loaned Vaani and me money, trusting us. I want you to know we have not betrayed your trust. We just don't have the money!"

Girish seemed relieved that he had been spared acrimony in the conversation. He was also perhaps surprised that I never asked, "How dare you bring the cops home?"

He replied, barely audible, his gaze on the floor, "Somehow AVIS, please pay me back. I need the money urgently."

I replied, "I realize that I am not only cashless but also unable to convince you that I am cashless. I cannot take cash from my living expenses and pay you Girish. Unless I survive you have no chance of recovering the money from me. So, I will keep this simple. Either trust me and wait or please do what you feel is right. I will not protest. I will not resist. Because I know what's compelling you to do what you are doing."

Then we both sat in silence. I studied the office in detail. Thick cobwebs hung from the ceiling. Used and sweat-stained uniforms dangled from clothes hooks on the wall. Some of the cops had left their brown regulation shoes and used socks behind. Registers and files towered on top of the tables. A black board displayed the year-to-date status of cases booked, investigated and solved at this station in the current year. A simple review of the data, last updated up to June 30th, revealed that there was a 30% resolution rate at this station. My eye caught a picture of Shirdi Sai Baba taped haphazardly on a cupboard. 'Shraddha' and 'Saburi'– Faith and Patience. His two-word gospel made profound sense to me at that moment. *I had to have faith and remain patient, even if this episode stretched over the weekend and into next week.*

I glanced at an old clock ticking away on the dirty wall. It was 12.30 AM. I thought about *Mom*. We must have been here for almost 90 minutes. And *Mom* was waiting outside. What was she doing? How was she coping with this situation?

Just then a constable walked into the room with my mobile phone. He said *Mom* wanted me to see something in it. As I opened the flap of my Nokia Communicator, I saw an unsent, open message window that read: "Spoken to Shankar Raman.[95] Help is on its way. Don't worry. Be bold." I had been feeling so powerless, so helpless; that message from *Mom* both reassured and energized me. I returned the phone to *Mom* through the constable and continued to meditate on that picture of Shirdi Sai Baba.

You both may not know this, but Uncle Shankar, a close friend of our family, is well-connected politically to the ruling party in Tamil Nadu. If he had been spoken to, it meant he would have someone speak to the cop heading the E4 Police Station and convince him that we were not in a position to make any payment now and that technically the cops did not have a role to play in this matter which was civil in nature. I was sure of the action that Uncle Shankar would initiate because Uncle Shankar knew the gory details of our bankruptcy and knew of each of our creditors, if not personally, at least by name. *Mom* and I had spent hours brainstorming with him as he had also been through a similar experience. He had reassured me and *Mom*, on more than one occasion, that if any of the creditors, particularly, the usurious high-interest lenders, used illegal

---

[95] Real name not disclosed to protect identity.

means to demand money from us, he would be available and willing to speak at the highest levels of the police force in Tamil Nadu and ensure that we were dealt with fairly and justly.

I silently celebrated *Mom's* presence of mind to call Uncle Shankar.

A little past 1 AM, the SI reappeared with Girish's companion in tow. Girish's companion was looking flustered.

He said to Girish, "The b#@*x$d has political connections."

Girish looked lost. But I knew that Uncle Shankar had placed his calls.

The SI sat down in his chair. He looked at me.

He smiled. "Sir, why are you in the position in which you are? You seem educated. You seem well-mannered. It gives me no joy having you come over to the Station like this and having your poor wife stand outside. What can we do to help you, Sir?"

I pretended not to notice the change in tone and the sudden respect the SI had developed for me. 'I know that Shankar has made his calls; he doesn't know yet that I know,' I thought. I responded cautiously, choosing my words carefully. My focus was that, independent of Uncle Shankar's efforts, I had to establish my credibility with the SI.

I said, "I am most grateful Sir, for your willingness to hear me out. *Fortune and tragedy do not choose time or income strata to strike.* You have seen enough of Life I believe, to know this.

My business has gone bust. I have not been able to pay rent for several months now for that apartment in Bishop Garden that I live in. My landlord has filed a case in court to evict me and my family. We have no cash to move out else we would have, sparing him the misery of having to proceed legally. I have every intention to pay my friend Girish here. I have amply demonstrated my intent by paying him interest at a humungous rate in the past and until such time that I had cash-flow. Now, I have no cash, forget cash-flow. Whatever I earn from my business, which is very low, compared to what we need, I use it to cover living expenses like groceries, school fees, phone bills, electricity bills and fuel, pay for staff salaries to keep my business going and for legal costs. I have regularly been in touch with Girish and several other creditors of mine, month on month. If you will allow me a moment I can show you what a mess my wife and I are in. I can show you all the details of our borrowings and all the emails I have written to various parties, including Girish. All that information is in my laptop. I want you to also know that this matter, in my opinion, is not criminal in nature, as my friend is making it out to be. It is a civil matter and he can proceed on those lines. I have promised him I will face it and when I am able to, return the cash to him with full interest and also compensate him for any legal costs. Despite my efforts to justify my position, if you are not convinced, then I request you to do what you deem right. I will face it with humility. But Sir, the chances of anyone, including Girish, getting any money out of me, are good only as long as I am out and free and am allowed to rebuild my business, one brick at a time. Keeping me locked up may soothe someone's ego but will help no one get money out of me and my Firm!"

The SI was clearly convinced. He said he did not want to see what was in my laptop though he said he was appreciative of me carrying it along.

He said to Girish now, much to my surprise, "Sir, I think you have to trust this man. I don't want you to think he has pulled any strings. Just as you pulled strings to come to me, he seems to have done so too. The call I received has only directed me to be objective. Normally, in such cases, the police have limited or no jurisdiction unless directed by a court. Also, I see many people who are willing to pay a bribe to get out of here. This gentleman seems honest. I barely know him but I trust him. Can't you trust your own friend?"

Clearly, Girish was feeling uncomfortable. His companion was clenching his fists and visibly seething with rage. The SI wanted me to write a letter to him saying I was willing to come in for further questioning if I was needed. I said I would not do so until checking with my lawyer. I offered to drop off the letter during the day today if approved by Uncle Vijayaraghavan. The SI tried to push his case. I said he obviously knew where I lived and since he trusted me, he should give me time until later to give him the letter.

He finally agreed saying, "I like your attitude, Sir. *You are broke but are not willing to run away. You are honest and are not embarrassed of being so. You have the ability to refuse what you don't want to do and yet have the ability to get your way.* Go home Sir. Get a good night's sleep. Your poor wife is waiting outside. Please drive safe."

That, it seemed then, ended another, dark episode in our lives. At least for the moment. It could have been painfully longer but I was not to know then that there was some more drama left as we walked out of the Police Station.

Girish and his companion reached the street first. I was walking behind them. As they passed *Mom*, who was rushing towards me upon seeing me come out, I noticed that Girish's companion stared rather obscenely at her. I didn't like it but decided not to protest.

Mom and I hugged each other. It was only for two hours that we had been separated but it seemed like two lifetimes! I was very proud of your *Mom* at that moment. Most Indian women consider it shameful if they are summoned to a police station. Others fear it. *Mom* had braved an over two-hour vigil and had also executed a strategy to summon help in the middle of the night, all by herself. *I felt blessed!*

As we stepped onto the street, *Mom* handed me my mobile phone and watch. I glanced at the time as I strapped on the watch. It was getting to be 2 AM. It was warm. Very warm. And the humid July night was suffocating. Although we are so close to the sea, on some nights, in summer, not even a leaf will stir in Chennai.

As we started to walk towards where our car was parked across the street, opposite the Police Station, a white SUV screeched to a halt behind us. The screech was vulgar, I thought, tearing up the still, humid, suffocating silence of that dark night. I turned to see what was going on. A few men jumped out of the SUV. They looked like *filmy* henchmen. Girish and his companion were talking to the driver of the SUV. The SUV was parked smack in front of the Police Station and in the middle of the street. Its headlights lit up the dark street for about a furlong or so. Girish called out to me. I gestured to *Mom* to proceed towards our car and turned back to walk to Girish.

"So AVIS, what's the plan? When will you settle?" Girish asked.

He wasn't acrimonious at all. He was plain concerned.

"As soon as I am able, Girish. Right now all I can say is it may take several months," I replied.

Girish's companion reacted violently and thundered, "You are an English-speaking, white-collar criminal. And you have the audacity to use political influence. You swine!"

I replied calmly, "Sir, I have said this to Girish and I will say it again. I have every intention to pay him back. I just don't have the means. I request you to let me handle this with Girish. He loaned me the money. I borrowed it. I stand accountable. I have always communicated proactively with Girish. I will keep him updated of progress or delay going forward..."

The driver of the SUV interjected discourteously, "You dog! You will not listen to us this way!"

He then looked at *Mom*, who was bathed in the light from the SUV's headlights, then looked at Girish's companion and threatened, *"Enna, Thookidallama?* (What, shall we take [kidnap] her?) Then this dog will come running with the money."

I had only seen such scenes in Hindi and in Tamil films. This was surreal. We were in front of a police station. The cop in charge had accepted that this was a matter beyond his jurisdiction. Girish himself was reconciled to the situation but the goons whose help Girish had enlisted to recover his money, were insisting on making a mess, threatening to take the law into their hands. *Right in the heart of one of India's largest cities? In front of a police station?*

I looked the driver of the SUV in the eye. I placed my right hand on the car's open front door. And spoke in a slow, measured tone, very unlike me.

"Thukkiduviya   nee?   Kai   vei   parkkalam. Seeviduven.   (You   think   you   can   take   her?

Try touching her... and I will slice you up.)"
I retorted.

I really did not know what got into me. I am normally forthright with my views and can argue a point or justify a position with élan and equanimity. But this was different. I was feigning violent aggression and doing it well. It may even have been utterly foolish. This was unbridled bravado and it should have been quite unnecessary. What Girish's goons were indulging in was unlawful and distasteful. They were unreasonable folks who would do anything to achieve their ends. Even as I was reviewing the consequences of my bravado, I noticed that my aggression had pushed back the driver of the SUV. He physically moved two steps back. Girish's companion too moved away and Girish himself looked completely lost.

I continued, "Listen guys. I am a victim of circumstances but I am not a cheat. You stay out of this. Girish gets his money when I am able. If you make a mess, I will fight your unlawful means every step of the way."

At that precise moment, the SI stepped out of the Police Station, an unlit cigarette between his lips. Shocked at seeing all of us posturing the way we were, his astute cop sense alerting him that something was amiss, he hastily walked towards us.

Girish's companion was preparing to say something when the SI stepped into our midst and said, "Listen guys. This is an order. You will have nothing to do with Mr. Viswanathan. He will pay when able. Just leave him alone."

He then looked at *Mom* and called out to her, "Madam, kindly take your husband home! Don't worry, *Saar*.[96] Don't worry, Madam! You are good people. Nobody will harm you."

We got into our car and drove back home. Once home, we had some green tea. Over tea, *Mom* and I reviewed the night's developments. Fundamentally, Girish had every reason to be aggressive and demand his money back. Perhaps the means he employed were unlawful. He was a friend alright but essentially someone who was a lender first and had then become a close friend. He had drawn good interest on the principal amount he had loaned us. While I was still baffled at his tactic of using a police-based collection mechanism, I held no grudges against him. He did what he thought was right.

It appeared to me and *Mom* that he had got our home address from your aunt's (my sister's) husband, who had incidentally once been a team member at our Firm and who had actually introduced Girish as a lender to us. Girish was not a typical lender. He had a fund which he had created based on bonuses, increments, ESOP[97]

---

[96] *Saar* – Tamil-accented usage of 'Sir'.
[97] ESOP – Employee Stock Option Plans, normally offered by Information Technology companies to retain employees

encashments, that he had been able to earn as a software engineer based in the US. He deployed that fund among 'trustworthy' friends for sizeable interest rates. I did not and will not challenge his rate of interest because I accepted it willingly. I will not challenge his actions because I believe he did what he thought was right. I have nothing against my brother-in-law if he indeed disclosed my home address to Girish because he too did what he thought was right! Everyone has their views about what they are doing and believes it to be right. Nothing wrong with that.

I am just happy *Mom* and I acted strategically and tactically. Strategically, by refusing to get intimidated by the police action and by choosing to be prepared to face 'whatever' action rather than agree to pay, when we have no cash. Tactically, by contacting Uncle Shankar, and to pay back the other party's tactic in their own coin! I could have 'brokered' an arrangement with Girish, offering to pay him a sum every month and therefore spared us this miserable experience. But what is the point in paying someone and not having money to run the family and meet our crucial necessities? I could have bribed the SI, if he was willing to take a bribe, and played one up on Girish and his cronies. But then the cop(s) would have tasted first blood and would keep wanting more and more. It would have started a cycle of endless tyranny. If we could possibly buy peace with such an action, it would have been worth attempting. But I would have lost my peace by doing that. Bribing would be unethical, unlawful and very unlike *Mom* and me.

Life will often place you in situations like the one we experienced last night. You cannot solve a situation by fearing it. You can only deal with it effectively, by facing it. Don't choose the easy way out by saying things which you don't mean or by saying things which are untrue or difficult to live by.

For example, a year ago, a government department slapped a claim of ₹14 Lakh ($28,000) on our Firm. Our auditor (a CPA) refused to represent us to meet the authorities because we had not paid the audit firm their fees in two years. *Mom* and I decided to meet the officer in the government department directly and explain our circumstances. The auditor, whose son studies in the same class as Aanch, warned us against 'putting our hand into a snake-pit' but we decided to go ahead. *Our reasoning: it was better to deal with the issue head-on than live in fear.*

We met the official concerned and while narrating our story, concluded by telling him that we were not even contesting the claim because we were not qualified to do so. We asked for his understanding and for time to pay up. *We said we can't pay now and we can't bribe.*

The official, in whom were vested sweeping powers to slap claims and effect collections, was surprised at our candour. He said that in his 30 years of service, he had never encountered such an honest and proactive approach or heard such a moving story.

"My heart goes out to you and your family, Sir. This is a department where people like you come to bribe people like me only after they have been coerced into submission by the department. When we forcibly summon people, they seek both illegitimate and often unreasonable, waivers. We allow them the waivers because that's how the system works. We threaten people and they cough up. But here you are, proactively coming and meeting me. I am moved by your story. Just leave. Forget about this claim. You have bigger things, like saving your family, to deal with," he told us, flinging the claim file for our Firm to a pile beside his desk.

Telling the truth as it is, however impractical and unbelievable it may seem, and by always choosing to wear my Life on my sleeve, has always worked for me. And for us. It has taught us that people always respect the truth and revere honesty.

What I want you both to learn from this experience is to always hold on to the truth, no matter what. Learn to face reality. Life is like darkness, the more you run away from it, the more it will haunt you; but if you face it, it will be bliss. As kids, we were all afraid of dark rooms. Or of stray dogs on the streets (especially in India).

As long as we feared the dark rooms, we were haunted even in our thoughts. That moment of bravado with the SUV driver was one where I faced up to a fearful reality and looked it in the eye. Had I allowed him to continue to threaten us, he would have exploited us. Not just last night, but forever. I could have told Girish too that I will pay him by next week or next month or next quarter and I could have bought peace with him and his people. I could then have saved everyone a few hours of time but that would have ensured that we never slept well in the future. We would have always been anxious, fearful and at their mercy.

Facing up to your oppressor(s) knowing that the truth is with you, in you, on your side, is like staring back at the street dogs. The moment we run from them, they start barking and running after us. If we were to just turn around, freeze and stare at them, they would whine and slink away. So, it is with Life's realities. Don't hide from them. Face them. When you face up to a situation, it will stop haunting you. Facing it may not change a situation but your fear will evaporate. Then you will just be left with reality.

When you say what you are feeling, when you wear your Life on your sleeve, you may make the situation uncomfortable and may even cause the person who created the situation some discomfort. But you will also always lead everyone concerned to peace and understanding. That's where you eventually need to arrive. Only the truth can lead you to peace. In the end what matters is peace. Just peace!

May The Truth Inspire You Too...
Dad

13

You Will Find Beauty In Unexpected Places!

"Witness the beauty in all that you meet."

~ Anonymous

Monday, February 4, 2008
7.00 PM: Chennai

Dear Aash and Aanch,

A dangerous underworld don, from whom we had borrowed money, taught me and *Mom* a valuable lesson today!

Saidapet Jaggu[98] is many things to many people. He is a land grabber who makes his millions through shady real estate deals. He is a shadow, what we call *benami*,[99] in India, for several politicians and ministers in Tamil Nadu's ruling clan. He also runs an efficient force of goons whom he offers, on a premium pay-by-deal basis, to help his 'nameless, faceless' clients recover money or property. These goons will threaten people with dire consequences if they don't comply or pay up or both. Jaggu also loans people money. He once told us, trying to sound virtuous, that the 'only thing he does not do is murder people'!

At the end of 2007, in that desperate last quarter, we borrowed from Jaggu. He came and inspected our office and then our home. He told me and *Mom*, while handing me the loan cheque, that he would not hesitate to hold one of us hostage,

---

[98] Real name not disclosed to protect identity.
[99] *Benami* – One who's a front in a shady business transaction.

till the other one cleared the payment in case we defaulted on any of our our EMIs for repayment. He sounded convincing and we remember coming away scared.

We somehow managed to pay the first two EMIs, out of the five, by borrowing from here and there. But we bounced the third one yesterday.

Promptly, Jaggu summoned us to his office this morning. His office is in one of the   bylanes of congested Saidapet. You enter a cheap commercial plaza and behind a shop selling coconuts in wholesale is a rolling metal shutter that is pulled up when you announce your arrival. It is a dark, hideous place. A chant in praise of Lord *Venkateswara*[100] was playing in the background from an old desktop computer. An assistant, with bloodshot eyes, informed Jaggu that we had arrived.

And Jaggu shouted out for me. "*Vaa, Iyer-e! Vaa!* (Come *Iyer*,[101] come!)"

He did not invite us to sit. I concluded that defaulters are not shown either mercy or courtesy. I explained our circumstances and conceded that we had made a mistake borrowing from him. He heard me out patiently. He then disturbingly kept playing with a metal paper weight, which kept

---

[100]Lord Venkateswara – a Hindu deity, Maha Vishnu, whose principal shrine is on a hill in Tirupati, in the South Indian state of Andhra Pradesh.

[101]*Iyer* – a Brahmin sub-caste in South India, especially in Tamil Nadu; to which AVIS and Vaani belong.

falling noisily back on his glass-topped desk every time he tried to make it spin like a top, while we stood in silence. After playing with the paperweight for a long time, he replied, "I have no reason to disbelieve you. But I need my money, *kannu*![102] Period! Or else..."

It was a cold-blooded threat. It sent a shiver down my spine. What he did not say, and which was left to our interpretation and imagination, was more intimidating than what he said.

I summoned all the courage in me, took a deep breath and with folded hands, said, "Sir, I want to humbly submit the following three points to you: 1. We should not have borrowed from you. 2. I hope you can give us some time and trust me and my wife. 3. We will not deliberately delay or deny you your EMI. But if we don't have the money where do we get it from? Also, if I start paying every single creditor who threatens me, I will have the whole city at my door. It's impractical. And we need to have a win-win arrangement."

What I said and the way I said it may have angered Jaggu but he didn't show it. He smiled wryly.

He continued to play with that paperweight even as he spoke. "I like the *dil*,[103] the audacity! You owe me money and you want a win-win to pay it to me? *Aha!* Sir, do you even know whom you are

---

[102]'*Kannu*' – is Tamil for 'honey', meaning, "I need the money, honey!"
[103]'*Dil*' – Tamil slang for guts.

talking to? The whole city shudders if it hears my name. Nobody dares to even stand in front of me. And you want a win-win?"

The paperweight fell down with an irritating clang, one more time. For a while none of us said a word. Only the chant kept playing in the background. Instead of making us feel its fervour, it added an element of eeriness to the situation.

Then, after what seemed an eternity, he spoke again, "You both are in a mess. I feel sorry for you. Let me tell you both that you must be bold. People will threaten you. They will come menacingly at you, but don't cower. Don't run away. Don't commit suicide. Stand and face the wolves. Remember you are being put through this experience for a reason. What the reason is you may not necessarily know now. But know that there is a reason which will manifest itself. You are a self-made man, Sir. I like your attitude. A self-made person is like a tree that grows because a bird ate a fruit and dropped the seed on the ground. The seed germinates and takes root through a natural process and finally grows into a strong tree. You try pulling out such a plant or tree and it will be a difficult thing to do. The plant's roots will be stubborn, strong and will refuse to budge. Whereas try pulling out a plant that you bought from a nursery and planted in your garden, it will give up easily when you yank it out.

"You both will emerge stronger through this experience. Mark my words. Go and work on your business. I will wait. But remember, when you are able to repay your loans, you should pay me first. In the meantime, if anyone torments you and threatens you with dire consequences, wanting their money back, tell them you haven't yet paid Saidapet Jaggu. Ask them how can you pay them when you haven't settled a ruthless devil called Jaggu? Go home Sir. Go home sister. May God be with you."

We couldn't believe our ears. Here was the most feared man in Chennai's underworld. We had heard that he was ruthless. He spared nobody, and here he was, not just giving us time, but giving us such a beautiful sermon on Life. *Mom* folded her hands in reverence. I reached out, held his right hand in both my hands and placed my forehead on his extended hand, as a salutation. I promised him that we would honour his trust in us.

This is Life. It never ceases to surprise you and amaze you. *In every moment you will find beauty, often in completely unexpected places.* I believe, more so thanks to this experience we are going through now, that beyond professional and financial considerations, when you have personal integrity, people do see it, feel it and connect with it. This is the most mystical, spiritual and beautiful aspect of being human. *Mom* and I must have invoked and established a soul connection with Jaggu. This made us see beauty where we may well have experienced terror!

This kind of soul-stirring experience is happening to us far too frequently. Last week, we were in a courtroom at the Metropolitan Magistrates' Court premises in Saidapet. As we awaited our turn outside, to be called in for our hearing, I stood, with my back to the wall, facing a stairway, leading up to an arch that opened up into the sky. Bright sunlight poured in through this arch. The sunlight created a divine spectacle of dust particles from the stairway floating in the air, descending to settle on the stairs and then being kicked up yet again with each pair of feet that walked up and down the steps. I couldn't help but see the beauty in that banal moment. These lines flowed through me and I captured the poetry on my mobile phone:

Courtroom Drama

Looking up the stairway,

Red-brick worn out walls by the sides,

An over-worn staccato handrail stared back in agony.

An arch that had seen many a stalwart, many a hapless citizen, many a hardened criminal and many a judicial luminary approach,

Seemed, of all things, inviting this morning.

It wore a seductive gleam today, as it let the sunlight, torrents of it, stream onto the stairs.

Climbing feet disturbed the dust particles,

They rose like weightless objects, dignified in flight,

Millions of them.

And as they struggled to land gracefully in the hope of settling

Somewhere on those steps,

More feet kicked them up.

The saving grace in this courtroom drama, a magnificent show of light, shadows and movement, was the sunlight that made,

These humble dust particles appear special, exalted, holy and celestial.

The irony was not lost on me.

It is with a heavy heart that those feet ascend or descend, it is with disdain that they stomp, it is in pain that they trudge, it is in victory that they dribble down.

Some win, some lose their battles here.

Unknown to them, the dust particles smile, their minuscule frames glowing in the fresh incandescent sunlight.

In glee they declare, ultimately, this step, this is every frail or menacing foot's last refuge.

The last station.

This stairway. Maybe to heaven. Maybe to hell. Maybe to this courtroom again.

But surely to dust.

Where we all came from and unto which we will all return...

Clearly, a courtroom, that too in India, is the last place for poetry. It can be depressing to even stand there amidst all that chaos. And yet I found beauty there.

I have tried to understand why I see beauty even in pain and in the most unlikely of places. I believe this is because I am beginning to treat everything in Life as just another event without trying to analyze it. With such a detached perspective, though I am not always successful in staying so, I am beginning to find peace within me and beauty around me.

This is how I believe it works. There is a cosmic design. And you and I are part of that design. You have your role to play as witness or as collaborator or participant depending on where you are at a precise moment and what you are doing. Each event or person is also a teacher. So you have yet another role to play, that of a student. You have a choice too – to learn from the event or person. The reason why people don't find the peace they seek so desperately is because they don't learn from people or events. Instead, they label events or people as good or bad. A cat crosses your path and you think it is 'bad'. A flower falls from an idol and you think it is 'good'. Most hotels in the US do not have a 13th floor because it is 'bad'. So when you do get a room that's numbered 13, you think it is 'bad'. You agonize over the 'badness' of the room and your poor luck and lose your peace. When we attach meanings and then label happenings or people, we begin to have expectations from them. So you expect an underworld don to be inhuman. You think that courtrooms in India are unkempt, dreary places where you will suffer and not where you will feel inspired. These preconceived notions and expectations ruin our peace.

Instead, treat each event or person as an opportunity to learn. Even if someone is causing you pain, you can learn what not to do from that person. The essence of Life is to soak in the learning and bask in the beauty of each moment, each experience. There's beauty everywhere and in everyone, provided you care to pause and see it.

To The Beauty In Each Moment,
Dad

14

Forgive, Even If You Can't Forget!

'Jesus said, "Father, forgive them, for they do not know what they are doing."'

~ Luke 23:34

Thursday, January 6, 2011
7.00 PM: Pune

Dear Aash and Aanch,

As I boarded my Kingfisher[104] flight to Pune this afternoon at 3 PM, and fastened my seatbelt, I pulled out my phone to turn it off. This text message arrived precisely at that moment (I have not corrected either the language or the grammar or the typos!):

"Happy new year upadte: Dad suffered a heart attack last Saturday. Both bro and I were on travel. He refused to get admitted for lack of money. Rite now he is alive. FYI! Do urself 2 favors: a) try and forgive urself b) pls don't cme anywhere closer to ur Dad! I mite jst burn u alive!!! God bless!!!"

It was an SMS from my sister, your aunt, to me.

Since I was the last to board, I had to turn off the phone immediately. I knew though, surely, that nothing was seriously wrong with my father, your Kasi[105] *thatha*, because I had spoken to him only a couple of days ago. My sister's reference to a 'heart attack', I believe, was an exaggerated view of events that had unfolded last weekend. My father had told me that he had gone through an

---

[104]Kingfisher – a popular airline in India at that time.
[105]Kasi – A Kasi Viswanathan, AVIS' father.

angiogram procedure to check for potential risks and had been advised that for his age and his chronic diabetic condition he was doing 'fine' and no further course of action was recommended.

This SMS was one more acrimonious missive, in a heart-wrenching series, from my siblings, and mother, who, for reasons best known to them, continue to believe that your *Mom* and I have cheated them and have 'blown up' the family property and all of my parents' wealth.

In the past I would rush to justify our actions and clear our name, but of late, I have learnt to forgive and move on. What I have learnt is that it may not always be possible to forget what someone says or does, but forgiving them will spare you grief and suffering, and free up your spirit, making you accept people for who they are rather than what you would like them to be!

I have learnt this the hard way though.

My sister is 10 years younger than me. I literally raised her in the first 10 years of her Life. Baby-sitting, taking her to school, teaching her the alphabet and, as she grew up, helping fulfil some of her adolescent aspirations that my conservative parents were immediately not supportive of.

My brother and I had a very good and close friendship. We never met daily, although we have lived, and continue to live, in the same city, Chennai, for over 15 years now. But like good friends, we laughed and shared our lives with each other every time we met.

In the last several years, owing to various inexplicable machinations by my mother, and my immature responses to them, my sister and I have become very distant from each other. In a Tamil Brahmin,[106] and *Palaghattan*[107] family, such estrangements are commonplace. But our bankruptcy, and attendant inability to repay money we have borrowed from my parents, has further complicated things in an already doubt-filled, vitiated and untrusting family environment. For one, my brother has severed all ties with me and us. And my sister from being merely distant has turned overtly hostile.

The reasons for an already fractious environment turning bitter are not difficult to understand. My mother, owing to her own insecurities, believes that your *Mom* and I have the money but have not been paying them back. They believe that we are earning a lot of money and that we are using all the money we earn to pay for Aash's University of Chicago education and 'living it up'. It is my belief that my mother may have planted a seed of doubt in the minds of both my younger siblings that we have cheated the family.

In July 2009, despite my fervent appeals, my mother decided to sell the family property that I

---

[106]Tamil Brahmin – caste in India, native to Tamil Nadu.

[107]*Palaghattan* – a sect of Tamil Brahmins who originate from the border district of Palakkad in the neighbouring state of Kerala, West of Tamil Nadu.

had mortgaged with the bank a few years ago to raise cash for our Firm. While the property was in her name, the mortgage was in our Firm's name. She used some part of the cash from that sale to pay off the bank and close the mortgage because that was the only condition on which the bank was going to agree not to legally proceed to seize the property and liquidate it on their own. My mother's logic was she didn't want my father or her to face litigation and eventual eviction. Fair enough. They were doing the best thing for themselves, given the circumstances.

But there was a problem. Though both my siblings were not convinced or supportive of my parents' decision to sell the property and move in with one of them, they refused to join hands with me to talk my parents out of their proposed plan of action. My brother and sister were already angry that I had 'cheated' the family and felt that the distress sale of a family property, in Gandhi Nagar, Adayar,[108] Chennai was foolish, given the way real estate prices were climbing just then. I got the impression that they were wary of my parents moving in with them to share their living space, till my parents purchased a new apartment for themselves on the outskirts of Chennai. Despite our similar perspectives, neither of them responded favourably when

---

[108]Gandhi Nagar, Adayar – a residential neighbourhood in Adayar, a prominent locality in South Chennai.

I wrote to the family on Thursday, August 20, 2009, appealing that we don't sell the property, and that we stay together as a family in this, trusting each other and taking a longer-term view for all concerned.

The sale of the property took place and we three children, me, my brother and my sister, were as good as mute spectators. My parents first went to stay with my brother and eventually divided their time between staying with my sister and my brother. For the first few months, my brother and his wife were possibly able to put up with my mother. My father should not have been an issue at all. He has his own outlook in Life but it is a least intrusive one. Whereas, my mother is just the opposite. Naturally, my brother and his wife must have faced problems having them stay with them.

So, my brother came to me with a proposition, which I thought, was logical *prima facie*. He said since my borrowing money and my inability to repay had caused this situation of my parents being 'homeless', I must shoulder the responsibility of providing a home for them. He suggested that I have our parents stay with us. I, however, refused to assume that responsibility. I said that while I was extremely grateful to my parents for having allowed me access to the family property documents and also for loaning us money, I did not appreciate their selling the property and settling my Firm's mortgage with the bank. I said I did not also appreciate him and my sister not supporting my efforts to talk our parents out of that plan. Further, I reminded him that my chemistry with my mother was non-existent. *We both could not stay under the same roof.*

I did not mince words. I had, and still have, no shame or guilt. Further, in the wake of all the challenges I was faced with, with creditors coming looking for me and *Mom* at all times, often adopting unlawful means to recover their dues, I didn't want my parents having to see and face any of that drama on a daily basis. I wanted to spare them the misery of that perpetual crisis-ridden state. More importantly, I did not want my mother opining on how we should be handling a bankruptcy. She was a great champion of me and *Mom* becoming Amway distributors or bagging 'training contracts' from government departments by pandering to the whims of *babus*.[109] She said both Amway and government contracts meant 'loads of money'. I agree that she perhaps was trying to be helpful and was thinking 'out-of-the-box'. But it is one thing to suggest, recommend, or advise and another thing to want to run someone's Life. I tried telling my mother that it wasn't my path to make money by any means but to do what gave us joy and profits. Whenever I said that, she would say that people who owed money to people did not have a right to pursue joy or be choosy about what they did.

"Don't be a fool. Do whatever it takes, make money, pay off your dues beginning with what

---

[109]*'Babus'* – In India, bureaucrats are called *'babus'*.

you owe me and then pursue happiness, joy, whatever..." she once told me.

She sounded pretty much like some of our creditors, but there was a difference. A relationship with a creditor can at best be described as professional and a disagreement is perfectly permissible. But when your mother becomes your creditor, and behaves coldly, then you know that you must be vocal and firm. I told my brother that my mother's interference would ruin my peace and I needed to guard my peace badly to wage, and *win*, this war, the biggest one of our lives so far.

I remember we sat at a corner table at the Café Coffee Day in Indira Nagar,[110] on Saturday, August 7, 2010, when we discussed this matter the last time, like mature adults. We were missing someone at that table though. We had invited my sister to join the discussion. Now, my mother, being manipulative in the way only she can be, wanted to join the meeting as well. I was insistent that we three siblings meet first, not even with our spouses, but just us. Whatever resolution we arrive at, I said, we would present it to our parents. I had initiated the discussions and wanted the family, including me, to bury the past and make a fresh beginning as responsible adults

---

[110]Café Coffee Day – an Indian coffee chain, one of whose outlets is in Indira Nagar – another residential neighbourhood in Adayar in South Chennai.

who would support each other in the years of opportunity, love and care that lay ahead of us. It is my understanding that because my mother felt slighted at my insistence that she stay out of the meeting, she may have influenced my sister to cite baby-sitting challenges and skip the meeting. So, there we were, my brother and I, with no resolution on the table that evening.

Something had to be done and quickly! That's when I proposed a simple, practical model that I strongly believed guaranteed peace and happiness to all concerned. I appealed to my brother inviting him to display leadership. I said I was broke. Not he or my sister. They possibly did not have huge cash reserves at their disposal, but they could put together a small corpus and move our parents to a small, rented apartment near their own residences in Adayar, Chennai. I said, although I didn't have cash just then, I would help everyone set up this infrastructure, help relocate our parents and would take care of sending their daily meals from my home to them. When I was able, I promised, I would repay the corpus that my brother and sister would have advanced. That way, since she loathed getting into the kitchen, my mother would be happy pursuing her career as an entrepreneur, social activist, writer and teacher and be able to do other things she loved doing. My siblings would not have to face any intrusions on their personal space. And I too would be free from having to deal with an unmanageable situation. I still believe it was a workable proposition but my brother shot it down. He said, he principally was opposed to me 'shirking responsibility' and that he would not advance any money to fund this project. Without him signing up, my sister too, I presume, because she never came and she never communicated, vetoed this idea.

I was left with no option but to accept the tags of 'cheat' and 'deserter' and 'opportunist' that my siblings pinned on me. Worse, they accused me of stooping to such abysmal levels of behaviour because they believed your *Mom* was influencing me. This is a very Indian thing. Indian families traditionally believe that daughters-in-law split their beautiful homes and take their dutiful sons away. Your *Mom* unfortunately has had to bear this cross for my regrettable decision to borrow money from the family!

As I got home after meeting with my brother, he sent me this SMS at 8.30 PM that evening: ***"Dear anand, you have cheated us and cheated parents in a very big way, not because of money but they way you are dealing with us. We deal with you as a family and you are dealing with us as a creditor. Do not repent after it is too late. Ah, might be you care a damm about it. Your parents tears will have to be answered, every drop of it!!!"***

I chose not to respond to that message. I had made my point clear. I was willing to support them. Not financially now but physically, yes. Not, however, at the cost of my peace. I was not being understood and the least I could do was not compound the issue by trying to justify myself. In justifying my stance, I would end up having to prove him wrong. Which meant the vicious cycle of mistrust would go on and on!

This afternoon's SMS from my sister is one more in a series of acrimonious communications that arrive with amazing regularity. When trust is lost, every action of the party in the dock, presently it is *Mom* and me, comes under scrutiny and judgments are passed ruthlessly.

On Wednesday, August 18, 2010, just ahead of a Talk I was due to deliver on 'Dealing with Change in Life', for 60 top managers of a global insurance company at Radisson Temple Bay, Mahabalipuram,[111] my brother sent me this message: ***"Having cheated parents you and your wife are enjoying your honeymoon in a five-star resort."***

I was heartbroken. The income from this two-hour thought-provoking Talk was to be ₹25,000 ($500). We had ₹3,000 ($60) cash with us. This cheque would allow us to send a small wire to Aash and survive till the end of that month. *Inspiring*

---

[111]Radisson Temple Bay, Mahabalipuram – a beach resort, 60 kms from Chennai; Mahabalipuram was a port city built in the Seventh Century by the Pallava dynasty in South India.

people when you are wounded, deflated, kicked and trampled upon is very, very difficult. Nothing cripples the human mind and heart more than a stab from someone you think of and call your own. We still had 30 minutes before my Talk was due to begin. I told *Mom,* I couldn't do it.

She gave me a hug first and then told me, "Forgive them *Dad.* They don't know what they are doing. If they feel good by causing us injury, so be it. Even if you are hurt, don't let it get to you, *Dad.* Unless you deliver an inspiring Talk tonight we are not going to get repeat business from this client. If we don't resurrect our business, we are not going to recover. And if we don't recover, how are we going to repay so many people, starting with your own parents? So, forgive him. After all, he's your brother."

I got up from the sofa in our room at the resort, into which I had sunk when I had got the message, took a deep breath, closed my eyes, meditated on my brother, summoning an image of his cherubic face as a kid into my mind and while imagining that I was giving him a hug, I forgave him. That act moved me. I quickly wiped away the tears as they welled up, walked the long distance to the banquet area at the other end of the resort, and delivered, what our client and *Mom* believe was, one of the most inspirational Talks of my career!

Forgiveness is freedom. It is liberating. It makes your spirit light. It may never change anything for those you forgive; for instance, my brother continues to believe I have cheated them, but forgiveness has helped me cope with the pain. I have learnt to understand that people say or do things which are distasteful because they don't have the complete picture and in most cases, they also don't want to know the full story.

In September 2010, when Aanch travelled to Kuala Lumpur and Singapore, with her close friend's family, who also paid for her tickets and stay, my brother sent me a text saying: ***"Son in the US, daughter in Malaysia, and parents in the dark after you have cheated them brilliantly!"***

It hurt no doubt. My dear children, when you become parents you will appreciate this dilemma better. How does a parent deal with a request from a child, who is barely 15, and wants to go on a vacation with her best friend and her family? Especially when the friend's father knows your situation and is willing to take care of all the expenses? Do we tell a 15-year-old that we are sorry, we are bankrupt and we must not be seen as indulgent? *I am bankrupt but that doesn't give me the right to deny my children their aspirations, especially when the benevolent Universe is taking care of them!*

I did not respond to that SMS from my brother that day or to other messages from him or to the one today from my sister. During the approximately two hour flight to Pune from Chennai this afternoon, I recalled how much I had evolved over the years.

How each incident of betrayal, misunderstanding and guile by fellow human beings has taught me a new lesson in forgiveness, every single time. I marvelled at how I have crossed the treacherous chasm, from grief and suffering to acceptance and peace, using forgiveness as the dependable bridge I could walk upon with my eyes closed.

Let me share one other instance that taught me how liberating forgiveness can be. On Sunday, October 2, 2005, all seven members of the team in our Firm's Bengaluru office, moved to join a Mumbai-based PR firm. I was in a review with my EA at the Park Sheraton Hotel's Cappuccino coffee shop in Chennai, when we decided to call our Bengaluru Operations Head, a young man called Suresh Rajput,[112] to clarify some plans relating to client delivery planned for the following week. Suresh didn't answer our call. We decided to wait and called him a couple of hours later. Drawing no response, we called another team member. Again no reply. And then another. And another. By 8 PM that evening it became clear that something was very wrong.

My gut feeling – I am very intuitive about what happens in our Firm – told me that all was not well. One of the strengths of our Firm's work ethic and culture was seamless communication – 24x7, 365 days! Seven people cannot be unreachable on the same day, at the same time, I reasoned.

---

[112]Real name not disclosed to protect identity.

The next morning, Monday, October 3, 2005, I flew into Bengaluru by the early morning Jet Airways flight. I drove straight to the office expecting to find the housekeeping boy ready the place by 7.30 AM, which was the normal practice. I kept trying to reach Suresh and the rest of the team members but to no avail. When I got to the office, the housekeeping boy was standing outside. He too had been trying to reach Suresh and the rest of the team because the Office Assistant, who normally came with the keys each morning, had also not showed up! About an hour later, after conversing with the building's security guard and the housekeeping boy, I surmised that my team members, led by Suresh, had been conspiring to join a company called 'something Rose'[113] in Mumbai. The housekeeping boy maintained that there had been a flurry of calls and conversations that Suresh was leading with the team and every time the name 'Rose' figured somewhere.

I Googled the relevant terms and discovered that 'Rose' was indeed the suffix of a large PR firm in Mumbai. The reality hit me hard. *My entire team had deserted me.* Suresh had been a favourite of mine and had recently got an increment and a promotion. How could he do what he did? Yes, in those years, salaries would be backlogged, but did an *en masse* desertion qualify as a legitimate

---

[113]Real name of the firm not disclosed to protect identity.

action to avenge any struggling entrepreneur's last, unavoidable refuge of delaying salaries?

My first responsibility was to restore normalcy to our operations in Bengaluru. We had three active, paying clients in the city. They were the last of the clients who were being phased out as part of our Transformation Blueprint. But a client is a client. For as long as you have committed to, you have to provide the service you promised and own the outcome. We flew in three team members to Bengaluru, while *Mom* volunteered to handle the two clients in Chennai single-handedly.

Once the salvage operation was in place, I took a flight to Mumbai on Wednesday, October 5, 2005. I drove straight from the airport to Mahim,[114] where the PR firm's office was located. I did not have a meeting set up but I was driving to meet the two men who ran this firm then. I barged into their office and angrily demanded to meet them. The receptionist, in the large, open cubicle office, tried resisting my unannounced and forced demand to meet her bosses. Perhaps because I looked business-like in a suit, I reckoned she could not be entirely dismissive of me. When she finally prepared to inform her bosses, she asked for my name.

"Tell them AVIS is here," I thundered in Hindi, with the swagger and authority of the angry young

---

[114]Mahim – a quaint business and residential district in downtown Mumbai.

man played so perfectly by the Big B[115] in many a blockbuster Hindi film of the '70s and '80s.

Maybe it was the tone, maybe it was my name, but no sooner had I finished the sentence, than a head bobbed up from a cubicle on my left. It was Suresh! He looked alarmed, ashamed and dumbfounded!

While Suresh looked at me in disbelief, two gentlemen emerged from a large meeting room, into which the receptionist had darted, the moment I had announced my name.

One of them extended his hand to shake mine and said, "Hello AVIS! I am Chetan Margabandhu.[116] I expected to see you but not so soon."

He then introduced the other gentleman to me as Subash Chattopadhyay,[117] who too was a director at their firm. I had known of the two of them and their website had enough information to prepare me for this meeting. Chetan was a Tamilian[118] and Subash was a Bengali.[119] Both of them had set up this firm a few years ago. Chetan suggested that we step out of their office and go get some coffee.

---

[115]Big B – Amitabh Bachchan, a super star in Indian cinema, is often referred to as the 'Big B'.

[116]Real name not disclosed to protect identity.

[117]Real name not disclosed to protect identity.

[118]Tamilian – one hailing from the South Indian state of Tamil Nadu.

[119]Bengali – one hailing from the Eastern Indian state of West Bengal.

They took me to an Irani[120] café, across the
street from the building which housed their office.
As they ordered tea, coffee and cookies, I started
to speak. I was surprisingly calm and very blunt
with what I had to say.

I said, "I do know what you have done. It is
very unfortunate that you did this to a fellow
entrepreneur. You could have told me you were
doing this and allowed me some time to let these
guys go. At least it would not have left me feeling
as betrayed and lost as I do now."

Chetan replied, equally matter-of-factly, "AVIS,
all is fair in love, war and business. We are all
in business to profit. I see nothing wrong in what
has happened. We met your team members. We
made them formal offers for them to join us. They
accepted those offers. Now, if they did not complete
exit and handing over formalities at your end, it
really is not our business."

I was angry but more than that I was upset.
Across the world, any company worth its salt
insists that relieving and exit formalities are
completed before people come on board. In fact,
most employers demand that employees submit
such relieving documentation. However, I decided
not to bring up that point. Instead I shared my
hurt. I told Chetan and Subash how hurt I was.
I said how we were down in the dumps with our

---

[120]Irani – a reference to a café set up by immigrant Iranians
in Mumbai.

business and how this was going to hurt us more. And I talked about our people processes and how much Suresh had learned with us, and how much he had earned. As I spoke, I choked several times and finally broke down. Subash, reached out, held my hand and advised that I calm down.

He offered me some water to drink and said, "I don't know how this feels but I can try to understand. I hope you are feeling better AVIS, having met us and saying what you have just said."

I replied, fighting back my tears valiantly, "Gentlemen, I see where you are coming from. If you get a readymade office with a well-trained team in Bengaluru overnight, then why not do what you did? But let me tell you, if someone, seven of them actually, can do this to me and my Firm, believe me, they can do it to you too! My only advice is for Suresh. If either of you or he is a gentleman, then you will advise him to call me and apologize. He's a young, upcoming manager. We don't want him thinking what happened is acceptable."

I saw no more point in that meeting. I had got what I had wanted to say off my chest. I stood up, wished Chetan and Subash the best, thanked them for their time and left.

For a month, I carried the hurt in me. Every time I thought of Suresh and his new bosses, a fresh wave of anger rose in me. Whenever that happened I was unable to concentrate on anything else but that. When you are stung by betrayal, are hurt by someone's senseless guile, you feel used, abused and discarded. I experienced those emotions, several times over, daily.

Then, one month after that meeting at the Irani café in Colaba, Subash called me. He said, he had advised Suresh to call and apologize to me. I was surprised they actually took me seriously but appreciated his call and thanked him for it.

Suresh called me the same day. I asked him, more as a feedback, than for any other reason, why he did, what he did, to me and to our Firm.

"I wanted to move up in Life and become successful. Honestly Sir, I did not see any scope for your Firm to survive. Hence I decided to move and take the others with me. I am sorry if I hurt you," he said, struggling to say what he actually did, often pausing to gather his thoughts or gauge my response, or both.

I replied, "*Beta,*[121] while I don't buy your logic, and believe totally that our Firm will survive and that you will regret having left it, I forgive you because you have shown humility in calling me. *Chalo, mauf kiya!*[122] Don't ever do this to anyone else in the future!"

Although I told him that I would forgive him, I was not actually sure then that I would ever be

---

[121]*Beta* – means son in Hindi, an affectionate reference to a younger person.
[122]'*Chalo, mauf kiya!*' – 'Okay, I forgive you!' in Hindi.

able to do that. But, in reality, I did forgive him and *it made me heal faster from within.* A few weeks after this episode and my call with Suresh, I heard that the firm he had joined had bagged a large media relations mandate in Bengaluru. I sent him and his two bosses a text message congratulating them on their client win. I was genuinely happy for them. Suresh was a capable young manager and I could picture him making the pitch and closing the deal. It was an important step in a young man's career, to head a team, lead a city's operations, be sought after by an established firm from Mumbai and to bag a new client within the first quarter of his joining them. It was a moment that called for blessings and not curses. All three gentlemen replied thanking me, with Subash calling me and saying he really, really appreciated knowing me, and looked forward to a long and fruitful association with me.

I felt good. A rare feeling of joy enveloped me. Now, when I thought of Suresh and his two bosses, while there was some pain, there was no suffering. There was a good energy in me that I wished would touch their lives too. As a Firm, we were getting out of the media relations business. In any case, I would not have had a need for Suresh and the six others in a few more months after their move. *I concluded that I was not against what they did but did not appreciate or accept the way they did what they did.*

This is what forgiveness will help you with. It will help you separate the perpetrator and the action.

Resent the act, fight it if you must, but don't hate the doer, the perpetrator. Because anyone who does anything does so only because they think it is right to do what they are doing. For instance, in all the years that we used a debt-based model to expand our business, wasn't I convincing myself and others that it was the only and right way? So, by that logic, I must be feeling guilty of landing our Firm and family in such a big mess. Or over years of fighting my mother's machinations, or immaturely handling her sinister designs involving separating me and my sister, I am equally responsible for creating the fractured family culture that you both and your cousins will inherit. But, I asked myself, how much longer should I carry this burden of guilt and anger? I decided that I could not anymore. I therefore learned to forgive myself!

I have learned that anger, resentment, guilt and hatred – whether directed at others or at yourself – are impediments to your progress through Life! Most people do things that are hurtful or wrong without knowing that they are making a mistake. They take the view that they are right and continue to hold on to that position, operating from and seeing the world from that viewpoint. So, to them, it appears that they are doing the right thing. In forgiving them, we are cleansing ourselves. Similarly, haven't you too operated with a self-righteous view of yourself? How many times have you wronged others? Sit down and make a list. You will be surprised to see that list getting longer with each incident you remember. You will not be able to complete that list even in a span of several days. When you believe you can recollect no more, seek forgiveness, in your mind, from each one that you wronged. Right from letting down a school buddy, to lying to your parents, to being rude to your teacher, to taking out your frustrations on others; for everything, big or small, seek forgiveness. As you do this, undoubtedly, you will feel miserable. You will begin to think of yourself as a mean, immature and insolent human being. That's when you must forgive yourself.

It's alright, we all make mistakes. So did you. Having done that, you will find it a lot easier to forgive others who have done similar things to you. After all, they behaved just the way you did, right? So, go on, give yourself the gift of forgiveness. When you forgive yourself and others, you will find peace, love and bliss.

It's been a long journey of learning and practising forgiveness for me. It doesn't make me forget what has happened to me in my Life. But it helps me remember everything with gratitude. Each experience has taught me to grow up and move on!

Remember Everything And Everyone With
Gratitude,
Dad

15

Serve Before You Think You Deserve

**"Don't ask yourself what the world needs.
Ask yourself what makes you come alive and
then go do that. Because what the world
needs is people who have come alive."**

~ Howard Thurman, American Author
and Philosopher (1899~1981)

Friday, October 12, 2012
11.00 PM: Chennai

Dear Aash and Aanch,

Today I met a gentleman called Raghu Srinivasan[123] who says I saved his Life three years ago!

It happened like this. One of the people from whom we borrowed money is an eminent CEO of a large publicly listed company based in Chennai. The updates, at least one each quarter, that I used to write to all creditors and friends, were often read by this CEO's secretary who obviously had access to his email. I knew her well because we had done business with this CEO's company and over the years, the lady and I had struck up a warm, professional relationship. She had also met *Mom* and you both socially. I had met her husband, Raghu, briefly, on at least one occasion. In September 2009, she called me asking for some time to meet both me and *Mom* at home, saying Raghu needed urgent 'personal and professional' advice.

When they came home, the lady introduced Raghu formally and his professional background to us. It appears that he had dabbled in many businesses and had lost money in all

---

[123]Real name not disclosed to protect identity.

of them. Over the last decade or so, Raghu's entrepreneurial endeavours had landed him in a ₹50 Lakh ($100,000) debt trap. Much of the borrowings, like us, were taken in a personal capacity, from both organized sources like banks and from unorganized, and therefore menacingly aggressive, lenders. Raghu confessed in that meeting at our home that he was scared, worried, and did not know what to do! His wife feared that he may be contemplating drastic measures like suicide. She said that she had read my updates to her CEO and had often wondered if what they were going through did not pale in comparison to what we were going through. Finally, she had convinced Raghu to come and seek our perspective in dealing with their crisis.

Mom and I were aghast to hear the story. For one, we could empathize completely with their plight. Second, we were disturbed at the thought that Raghu would consider giving up on Life for just a ₹50 Lakh situation. Our own burden was 10 times bigger!

Almost immediately, we set out to draw up a blueprint for Raghu and his wife to come out of this situation. I began, however, with the following preface: "Guys, the first and most fundamental principle is to see reality and accept it. Next, please know that you will get out of this. How long it will take, can't be said right now, but this too shall pass! During this time, your first and *only* priority must be towards the two of you and your daughter. Monthly living expenses have to be met. Your daughter's basic needs and simple aspirations, as any teen can have, have to be the highest item on your to do, to provide list! Your creditors will have to wait. No matter what! Whatever your creditors do, whether they threaten, coerce, initiate legal or police action, whatever they do, do not pay any of them anything from your living expenses budget. You will have to wait for your business to grow and pay your creditors only when you have cash beyond your living and business operating expenses!"

When I finished speaking, I suddenly realized that the strategy outline had simply flown through me effortlessly. It seemed to me that something, someone, deep within me had spoken. It wasn't me! *Mom* described the extempore exposition as a confluence of experience, expertise and emotion!

"Because we are living this experience, it didn't appear like you were saying anything to just make a statement. You were prescribing, inspiring and leading, all at once," she later told me.

Over the next six months following that meeting, we led Raghu and his wife, to appreciate the simple strategic framework of taking care of yourself first, before paying your creditors. It is the same principle that every airline champions before take-off: 'In an emergency, please place the oxygen mask on yourself before helping another passenger.' It wasn't easy, because just like we kept running away from the problem in the initial stages, they had too. However, with effective counselling, and sharing our own experiences and learnings, we got both of them to understand that there was no other way. Slowly, as they became more and more capable of handling the situation themselves, we let them be.

Today, Raghu reported that they too had found a way to live with the problem, leading a Life of dignity and happiness, even while exploring newer ways to stabilize income, grow earnings and eventually retire the debt.

"The most important thing we learned from you and Vaani is to carry on living in spite of the problem. When I first met you at your home, I was so defeated and thought it was all over. Now I realize how myopic I was. Thank you AVIS! You saved my Life! You saved my family!" gushed Raghu, holding my hand for a long time, when we bumped into each other at a *satsang*[124] today.

Words cannot describe how *Mom* and I feel just now. It is very uplifting to know that you have touched and inspired someone. Money will come and go but your ability to make a difference to even one person in this big, beautiful, bountiful world is what counts.

The meeting with Raghu and his wife and their ₹50 Lakh debt situation opened myriad

---

[124] *Satsang* – a community prayer event.

possibilities for *Mom* and me! We started to seek out and remain available to handhold families and businesses going through similar experiences. We know exactly how it feels and we know, thanks to this experience, that it is imminently possible to live with unpaid debt in your Life. We have built this mentoring piece into our portfolio of services that we offer to the Universe – without any commercial considerations.

Actually, much before this mentoring opportunity came about, the night after that shameful meeting with my parents on Monday, May 4, 2009, when I was charged with attempting to assault my mother, *Mom* and I decided to stop wanting anything! I recall sitting in our bedroom and telling *Mom* that all I need is peace.

"I don't want money. I don't want to bounce back. I don't want to become a global Firm. All I need is peace. I am willing to do anything for peace!" I declared, with complete disregard for our present condition, as well as a profundity that only the inscrutable ways of Life can imbue in a person.

I was disgusted for several reasons. The business was just not picking up. There was no money. The final nail in the coffin happened to be the title of 'cheat' that my mother had bestowed on me earlier that evening! I was feeling worthless and defeated. *Mom*, though she was stronger than I was at that moment, shared my sense of dismay and hopelessness.

Six months prior to this conversation in our bedroom, we had had a similar one. This was on Friday, November 28, 2008; immediately after the 26/11 attacks on Mumbai's landmarks, The Taj Mahal Hotel and The Oberoi Hotel.[125] We both felt agitated, as every Indian was, over our helplessness in the wake of those dastardly attacks on our country and innocent citizens.

"Is there no way we can as Indians do anything about what's going on?" I had asked *Mom*.

It was a question asked from feeling completely hopeless for our motherland. Then, as happens with every well-meaning thought and intention, any effort to answer this question too died in infancy, drowned in the sea of everyday miseries called 'Business As Usual' (BAU).

In our case, BAU meant cashlessness along with hopelessness. Where do we begin? Do we begin fixing our lives or our nation? The very fact that we are even thinking of doing something beyond our immediate circle of income, interest and influence, and thinking of the country as a whole, indicated to *Mom* and me that we were slowly turning selfless. This altruistic stirring was cleansing and inspiring but it made us both feel disenchanted with 'normal' Life! When we attended social dos we found the conversations

---

[125]The Taj Mahal Hotel and The Oberoi Hotel – two of India's premium hotels, both located in Mumbai, and both of which were attacked by terrorists on November 26, 2008.

too shallow to merit participation. Over endless drinks, people spoke about the fluctuating fortunes of the share markets; the insecurities fuelled in them by the Great American Recession; the avarice injected in them by the real estate business; how they unfailingly succumbed to the irresistible temptations of climbing gold prices; and on the obscene scams hogging headlines in India! All of this seemed banal and uninteresting to us.

I had often, over long walks, told *Mom*, "Here we are struggling to find cash to survive and people have the time and temperament to indulge in such fruitless conversations?"

I never meant, nor do I mean now, any disrespect to those who enjoyed such discussions. It was simply that *Mom* and I were gravitating towards answering a more profound question: *What is more important in Life – living or 'earning a living'?*

We may have never asked this question had it not been for our bankruptcy. And we may never have found the answer, had it not been for the discussion in our bedroom on the night of May 5, 2009. I remember telling *Mom*, in a sudden 'eureka' moment, that what we needed to do was flip the paradigm.

I declared, "We are thinking in a very linear fashion. We expect Life to solve all our problems, give us money, help us repay our debt and then, we believe, we will do something for people, our society and our country. That may well happen, *Mom*, but it could take a long, long, time! *I think, instead of asking how we can make money, maybe we must ask ourselves – how can we be useful? Instead of saying we deserve more from Life, maybe we should ask, how can we serve?"*

I am glad I said what I did, though the inspiration came from a workshop I had co-anchored with my dear friend and mentor, whom you both know as Uncle Raja Krishnamoorthy. Raja *Saheb*, as *Mom* and I fondly call him, had used a PowerPoint slide titled '*Serve to Deserve*' in the workshop. That thought had stayed with me and undoubtedly served as an inspiration at that moment! I am also glad *Mom* immediately agreed. I believe both of us came to this conclusion from wanting inner peace and wanting to be useful rather than wanting to rid ourselves of our problems or wanting to be more successful!

We decided to implement our 'Be Useful' philosophy immediately. Two days after the resolution was made, on Thursday, May 7, 2009, *Mom* cooked a nice hot meal at home. She made *bisibelebath*[126] and packed it in five disposable meal casseroles.

Thursdays, as you know, are observed as special days for prayers to Shirdi Sai Baba. One of the

---

[126]'*Bisibelebath*' – a meal of rice, lentils and tamarind juice and spices; the recipe is native to Karnataka, a South Indian state.

simplest practices that Baba taught his followers was the power of feeding people. All his temples across India and the world feed the hungry, daily or weekly. During his lifetime Baba is believed to have cooked meals personally for people who visited him daily. Swami Sathya Sai Baba followed this practice diligently at Puttaparthi subsequently.

We decided to create our own process though. We committed to feeding five strangers on the street each Thursday starting that week. The criteria to qualify as a beneficiary of our service was that the person had to be homeless, hungry and a complete stranger to us. On that Thursday, we drove around the block and over a few blocks at lunch time and located five such people: hungry, lonely and desolate, on the streets. Each time we spotted someone; one of us would get down and hand over the meal, with some drinking water to wash it down. While doing this, we paused to look into the person's eyes, and thank her or him. *After all, that person, at that moment, was giving us an opportunity to be useful. In each encounter, we rediscovered what it means to be human.*

Over the weeks, we were humbled each time we did this. We realized that our problems are miniscule compared to what millions face daily. We began to feel blessed. What started off as a weekly practice in May 2009, became a daily one from July 2, 2009, Aash's birthday, and continues to be so even now! While we don't always cook the meals we distribute daily, at home, we source a meal for ₹50 ($1) each from a good, hygienic neighbourhood restaurant.

Encouraged with our ability to successfully implement and sustain this practice of being useful to the Universe that has given us the gift of Life, *Mom* and I decided to expand our scope of impact. A few years ago, in 2002~2003, the Rotary Club of Chennai Kilpauk[127] had invited me to partner with them and lead a Rotary Youth Leadership in Action (RYLA) Program camp at the Thiru Vi Ka School in Shenoy Nagar,[128] Chennai. It was a government-aided school, which served children from deprived and underprivileged backgrounds. It was led by one of the finest educationists in our country, K. Sivanandan. The year the RYLA intervention began, the school reported a pass percentage of under 30%, up from 25% the year before. Over the years that the school partnered with Rotary in the RYLA Program, Sivanandan led the school to report a 70% pass percentage. My role was to annually deliver an inspirational workshop for the students attending the RYLA camp.

After a few years, owing to both our challenges and the Rotary Club's revised priorities, the partnership came to an end. *Mom* and I however had great faith in Mr. Sivanandan and decided to meet him in an effort to serve more. We proposed to

---

[127]Rotary Club of Chennai Kilpauk – a Rotary Club in Chennai affiliated to the Rotary International movement.
[128]Shenoy Nagar – a residential area in central Chennai.

conduct a year-long 'Life Skills Lab' programme for students of classes IX and XI of his school to help them acquire critical Life skills. The programme would primarily expose them to defining and pursuing a Vision for themselves. Sivanandan spontaneously agreed. So, for two academic years, between 2009 and 2011, our Life Skills Lab sessions ran every other Saturday at the Thiru Vi Ka School. We taught about 60 children each year about how to identify and pursue Purpose, how to dream big, how to define a Vision for their lives and careers and how to work to a disciplined plan of action while staying rooted to their Values.

These children came from broken homes, or had been abused or deprived of a decent childhood and spoke little or no English. But they all loved the programme and the exposure we gave them. Uniformly, they all vowed, in their individual Vision descriptions, to eradicate corruption, poverty, poor hygiene, tobacco and alcohol when they grew up – all of these were scourges they had to live with daily! We taught them to set up email accounts in their school's computer labs, to open Facebook accounts, surf the net and express themselves online, in simple, working English. Each year's batch benefited greatly from the effort. We picked up two students, one from each year, based not only on academic excellence, but also on overall creativity, expression and leadership potential, and awarded them a scholarship in memory of your grandmother, *Mom's* mother, Padma *paati,* to pursue any educational course that they chose, in order to achieve their Vision.

To *Mom* and me, this was an extremely gratifying experience. *We realized that while we were financially bankrupt, intellectually, imaginatively and emotionally we could be useful!* We would have loved to continue this experience and experiment into a third year but Mr. Sivanandan retired from the school in the summer of 2011 and we were not confident the new principal understood what we were capable of doing there.

To be sure, the Life Skills Lab was a modest experiment. It is an idea that was born out of the 26/11 catharsis that all Indians experienced and the resultant awakening, in *Mom* and me, that if India must transform, Indians must transform. We need leadership in this country. I know attempting to coach and mould two leaders in a population of 1.2 billion Indians seems hopelessly inadequate. However, our endeavour is not to make a grandiose statement of intent or a visible splash with no follow-through. To have made a beginning, to be useful and to serve is more than enough. Most importantly, as we have discovered, we did not need money to serve. We just needed inclination, intent and initiative.

While the practice of feeding people daily and the Life Skills Lab experiment thrived, we were also energized with the progress we made with Raghu and his wife. Over the months following our meeting with Raghu, we began working with a young lady who runs a gym. She came to us unhappy, lost and mired in debt. There was an unmistakable sadness in her which she could neither conceal nor get rid of. She was breaking up with her husband and had two young children to take care of. She came to us asking if it was even worth living; forget attempting to solve her situation! Again, over several months, we were able to help her understand that the key to finding happiness is to be happy *despite* your circumstances. That it is only through being happy that you can find ways and means to set right the other aspects of your Life. *While success does not always guarantee happiness, happiness, always, over time, will deliver success.* In the past year, we have also helped a husband-wife duo, first generation entrepreneurs, who were struggling with a similar situation in their business, which was, sadly, also taking a toll on their marriage. In six months of leading, coaching and inspiring, their company has turned cash positive, has reported profits for the first time in five years, and the two have found new meaning and rediscovered the romance in their 12-year-old marriage!

As I write this, I am reminded of a call I placed at the end of January, 2008, to my first cousin C. P. Shankar, whom we all call CP, in Washington D.C. Though we got along well, CP and I have never really stayed in touch. I had visited him once in 1995 when I first went to the US. We thereafter met very infrequently at family events. In January 2008, he visited India to escort his father to go live with his family in the US. On that visit he and his wife Rama came home and had coffee with us.

As they were leaving, CP, who is an angel investor and runs a very successful tech enterprise in Silicon Valley, said to me, "Call me, okay? Let's not stay aloof. I am your brother. Treat me like one! When Aash comes to the US, tell him to call me. Whatever we can do, we will do for him!"

It was a very comforting offer. As you know, those were the early weeks of our bankruptcy. Each day was a new challenge. Each night had to be survived. One such sleepless night, I remember, was Republic Day, Saturday, January 26, 2008. Around 1 AM, unable to sleep, I called CP. I told him our story and said I would send him an Investor Memorandum and asked if he would consider being a white knight and invest in our Firm and if he would bail us out. CP was direct, blunt and to the point. At that moment he sounded the least bit inspirational.

He said, "Brother, I cannot be investing in your debt. I can be a part of your future though. But unless you take care of your debt, you can't build your future. It is a very interesting, awakening, learning phase that you are about to get into. Don't look for white knights. Don't seek investment. Live and deal with the situation. It will teach you something. I foresee you teaching people how to deal with a bankruptcy and how to come out of one. Make this phase a celebration of your Life! Wish you and Vaani all the best!"

I recall putting the phone down on him and wondering what an unbankable cousin I had, one who professed help but finally gave none! I was not bitter with him that night. Just confounded! Now, when I look back at that call, and all that I have shared with you both, I can't help but say that CP was both wise and prophetic. Or maybe he was ordained to say what he did and I was ordained to hear what I did!

This is what is tragic about us humans and what is beautiful about Life! *The beauty is that the Universe, gives us signs of what's coming all the time, and the tragedy is that we miss the signs, every single time.* We are so caught-up in this self-conceived, self-centred craving that we 'deserve' this or that; we completely miss the opportunity to serve. I am grateful to the Universe that *Mom* and I, albeit through sheer accident or cosmic design, rather than by personal will, found meaning by serving and being useful! We found that each act of service made us come alive and feel the soul within us connect with the ones of those whom we served. We felt alive, useful and blessed.

I want you both to feel alive too. Learn to live your Life like a candle in the dark. Let me share what I have learned about and from the inspiring metaphor of the candle. You may be burning down, with each passing day as you walk towards your death, but know that you can burn bright till your last breath. A candle signifies light. Light can take away any darkness. Darkness cannot make light fade away. Besides, a candle can light thousands of other candles – millions – without ever losing even a bit of its own brilliance, radiance and potency. Such immense possibility exists for all of us, you and me: to *give*, to contribute and to serve. Without losing anything we have. Yet we, somehow, seem to forever live in insecurity, worrying about melting away, thereby losing the opportunity we have to make a difference. Shel Silverstein's 1964 children's book *The Giving Tree* taught the world the power and meaning of giving. *To serve, as I have understood, means to give what you don't have to give, what you don't need to give, but you still give because you want to give!*

Instead of asking our all-time favourite question, 'What's in it for me?', or lamenting that 'I deserve', if we are ready and willing to give of ourselves – our time, our ideas, our efforts; if we can simply serve, Life assumes a new hue. We discover a sense of Purpose. The human race's eternal quest is to find peace and joy. We are continuously searching (and this is one search that Google cannot help with!) for meaning to and in our lives. The reason we keep searching and never find that meaning, that evasive peace, that elusive joy, is because every effort we are willing to make is counter-validated by the expectation of something in return. Instead of being in expectation mode, if we can put ourselves in 'ready to serve' mode, doing what will bring us alive, regardless of what benefits will accrue or what challenges we will face, we will find the peace that we have always searched and yearned for.

Serve, Doing What Brings You Alive!
Dad

Afterword

**"Life is a hard teacher. She gives the test
first and the lesson later."**

~ Anonymous

Dear Reader,

Vaani and I are humbled by your interest
and patience with our story. By picking up
this book and by getting to this part, the
Afterword, you have given us the opportunity to
share our learnings with you, just as we have done
with our children, Aashirwad and Aanchal. We will
always remain grateful to you for this opportunity.

While our story may seem unique and intensely
personal to Vaani and me, the learnings from it are
in every sense universal and can apply to anyone,
anywhere, in any situation.

You will have realized through knowing our story
that when we woke up to our bankruptcy, we too
were gripped by fear, anxiety, uncertainty and worry.

I lived through much of 2008 and 2009 recollecting, often several times daily, that horrifying scene from the Hindi film *Shaan*[129] (1980), where Shiv Kumar, the honest police officer (played memorably by Sunil Dutt), is chased down by over 50 of the villain's blood-thirsty hounds on an isolated beach, somewhere on an uninhabited island, off Mumbai. I had seen the movie as a 13-year-old. That scene came to haunt me 27 years later. I imagined that our 179 creditors, as it initially appeared to me, were gunning for me and Vaani. We were running faster and faster, but it seemed to be an exercise in futility. We thought then that we would eventually be chased down too. You will find, through my admission of me or Vaani crying in several instances cited in the book, that we too were vulnerable, helpless and every bit human. But as we progressed through our experience, we evolved as individuals and awakened to a different and beautiful way of living. We discovered that these 179 people were angels, not terrorists. We discovered that integrity of Purpose was more important than money; and wearing your Life on your sleeve and facing Life is better than running away from it. We learned that in any situation, you must, unfailingly, do what you can and what is possible.

It may not always be the right thing to do from another point of view but if you think it is what is possible, given the circumstances, and it doesn't

---

[129] *Shaan* – meaning 'Glory', directed by Ramesh Sippy.

disturb your inner peace, and you believe the outcome will be in the interests of all concerned, just keep the faith, and do what you must! This experience has taught us that it is indeed possible to live in this world, to be caught in worldly conflicts and attachments, and yet be above it all and maintain a spiritual, detached approach. Without doubt, my daily practice of *mouna* has helped me immensely in staying anchored and detached, aware and mindful. This means that every time fear or worry surface, as they always did, something from within me reminds me to calm down, to have faith and to be patient.

In the end, as we have discovered, intelligent living is pretty darn simple.

Let me leave you with a few simple principles that have helped us live, and experience happiness, despite years of financial distress and unimaginable uncertainty. These are lessons that Life has taught us over these seven years. You may want to apply them to your own unique Life situation and, miraculously, you will find they appeal to and are relevant in your context as well.

There's No Logic To And In Life! Just Magic!

Life has a mind of its own. The problem with the education we have received is that we are encouraged to think rationally, logically! This has made us believe that we are in control. 2+2 = 4. We know that. But sometimes in Life, 2+2 will *not* add up to 4! Despite your best intentions and your hard work and integrity, things will go wrong. You will be put in the dock. You will be challenged emotionally, physically and financially. At such times, it is best not to come in Life's way. Just go with the flow! Your intelligent, educated, human mind will tell you that you can try and control things. That you can swim against the tide. Sometimes it does work that way. But often, Life overtakes you! Then, nothing other than Life's designs may work for you. Just as it has happened to us.

People often ask us, wasn't taking up employment an option? Wasn't going back to my parents or siblings and brokering an arrangement, where we didn't have to pay rent or face eviction, an option? Wasn't educating Aashirwad in India an option? Wasn't trying a new line of business an option?

We agree that they all were options. These and many, many more were considered. Several were explored. Others were even attempted. But none of these options fell into place. None? Yes. *None.* It is bizarre, but true.

What we have come to conclude is that, while money matters, and can buy you things that may make you happy, it can never guarantee happiness. Isn't that pretty illogical? The truth is there is no logic in Life, to Life. Just Magic! Nothing that's happening to you, to me, to anyone out there, has any logic.

One of the most inquiring minds of the 20th and 21st Centuries, the renowned theoretical physicist, Stephen Hawking, has a motor neuron disease related to amyotrophic lateral sclerosis, a condition that has degenerated over the years and has rendered him completely paralyzed. He now communicates only through a speech generating device. Is that logical? Yet see how he copes with his Life, still astounding us with his brilliance. Well, that's magical!

The harder you work, the lesser you earn – at least the ratio is disproportionate to your level of work ethic and integrity. And those who have shallow value systems end up making all the money. Is that logical?

You don't smoke. You don't drink. But you still have a form of cancer which is rare and you only have six more months to live. Is that logical?

You have done no harm to anyone. All you wanted was a child. But she is born with muscular dystrophy. Is that logical?

Logically, by the theory of aerodynamics, the humble bumble bee cannot and must not fly. But magically it does. Perhaps, as they say, because it doesn't know it can't fly!

Look around you. Everything is illogical. Every story of human endeavour and survival defies logic. Yet, thanks to all your scientific conditioning, you imagine that you must approach Life logically. That if something is wrong or going wrong, it means you are finished. And time and again, you, all of humanity, has been proven wrong. It is never over until it is over. That's where Life's magic comes into play. Our experience has taught us that this inscrutable cosmic design clearly works more on magic than logic.

So, in essence, it is better to stop thinking logically about Life. Where reason stops, the soul takes over. The soul is nothing but the universal energy, which created and powers this Universe, inside you. When you connect with the soul, magic happens. You don't connect with this energy; you don't see who you really are – be whom you are really capable of being – because you try to operate through your intellect; mathematically, logically. That's where you miss the bus. Logic gives you the feeling that you know, that you are in control. But what happens when you rupture a heart valve; when a child dies; when a perfectly sound business is converted into a debt pile despite having the best standards of ethical governance and the best brains with you; when justice is denied to you by the highest court of the land; when a person you loved and cared for deeply, betrays you? When all these, and more, unpredictable, unfathomable situations – that you think happens to others and will never happen to you – become a reality in your Life, you will stop logic from stepping in. You will surrender to Life's magic. You will then tell Life, "Come, take me!" When you do that, believe me, you will truly see magic happening in your Life! Just as Vaani and I have seen and I have shared in this book!

Don't Come In The Way Of Your Children!

Fundamentally, we hope you will recognize and learn from our experience that the destinies of our children are not necessarily linked to our own.

I can't help but recall here what I have learnt from Khalil Gibran's brilliant insight: 'Your children are not your children. They are the sons and daughters of Life's longing for itself. They come through you but not from you, and though they are with you, yet they belong not to you.'

As I have confessed, it is but natural as parents, for us to worry about the welfare and security of our children. But when such worry comes in the way of their lives, their own explorations, their adventures, their falling down and learning their lessons – just as you and I did, the hard way – it would be grossly unfair and unjust.

Parenting, as Vaani and I have discovered, involves leadership. And a cardinal principle of leadership is letting go. I shudder to think what would have happened had we not sent Aashirwad to the University of Chicago. Not that he would not have graduated. He has a brilliant mind and he would have done well anywhere. But not sending him to Chicago would have meant denying him myriad opportunities. How else in India could we have provided for Aashirwad to get an opportunity to get face time with the top economists in the world, Gary Becker and Roger Myerson, and be taught by Steven Levitt? How else could we have built that kind of character, of facing not only the harsh winters, but to thrive in a multicultural environment in the wake of so much uncertainty over his being able to continue at the world's elite school for Economics, quarter upon quarter? How else would he have been able to witness Bill Gates speak live or walk the same halls as a number of the most incredible intellectuals, CEOs, heads of state and change-makers who visited his campus in the four years he spent there?

As a Life Coach, an organizational transformation consultant and as someone who teaches managers globally to lead, own and deliver, the common gaps I notice, and encourage organizations to fill, relate to people's inability to deal with change, uncertainty and finding opportunity in crises. Why would I deny my own child this learning – *live*, on the centre-stage of Life?

Our humble submission to you is, you must trust your children and their aspirations for themselves. My mother never trusted me and I know the pain of a child whose parent does not trust him. Even when your children are taking decisions, which in your opinion are debatable or questionable, while giving them your perspective, tell them that you trust them. Invite them to come celebrate with you if they pull off what they plan to do. Let them know also that if they fall down, failing in their attempts, they are most welcome back home. That with parents, there's no shame. There's just sharing. Never let your parental anxiety about your Life, your financial situation, your insecurities and fears over your relationships, lead you to cripple your children and impede what they have begun visualizing for themselves.

They may be inexperienced, naïve, if you will, but they are not stupid or foolish. Trust their Vision for themselves. The other day, I was talking to a parent who said she had discouraged her child from pursuing a career in film-making because she felt she had enough artistes in the family. Her husband is a famed, yet financially challenged artist. Another parent told me that he was worried about his daughter going to the same college as a boy with whom she had had a break-up. The break-up had a negative impact on her final semester of school. The child, on the other hand, was insistent on facing the situation and by doing that wanted to prove a point to herself, to her once-boyfriend and to the world that she was no pushover. In another such case, one set of parents kept the keys to the safe at home hidden because they didn't want the child to 'steal' money although there had been *no* such attempt by the child. Every time you think of your child, just ask yourself, if you would like to be, or would like to have been, treated like that by your parent. And even if you indeed were treated that way, there really is no need to continue the trend. You don't want your child to go through the same pain as you did, do you?

Bringing up children is simple if you treat them as adults. Empower them with choice, encourage them with trust and energize them with the view that every experience will teach them something. More than a parent, try being a teacher to your child. By taking decisions for them, by snooping on them, by making them live your Life, you are crippling them. The last thing you want is a weak leader in the future. Yet by worrying for your child you may end up creating just that! Trust is the fine line between fear of what might happen based on your own past experiences and the spirit of adventure that your child yearns for and so truly deserves. Walk that tight rope. That's your parental responsibility. Don't abdicate it. Discharge it fully! Remember, if you want your child to become a fine human being – and beyond that you must aspire for nothing – you must trust your child too with wanting to become one!

Having said all of that, I must confess that Vaani and I took a conscious call not to share the explicit details of our situation with our children for much of these last seven years. Not that we would want to deny them the learning – which is the essence of all the notes that I have written to them, a few of which have led to the creation of this book! We only withheld information for the immediate present, beyond what was evident, because we felt they wouldn't have been able to contribute in any way to solving the problems we faced. On the contrary, over-communication on our bankruptcy with them in real time would have led them to curtail their own imagination and limit their individual aspirations, thinking that they should not be burdening us to fund their dreams. Yet, when he graduated, I sat Aashirwad down and, over several nights and pegs of whisky in Chicago, shared with him (also having him read my journal notes) what we had been and are continuing to go through. I told him that I trusted him to get stronger by hearing our story and not feel guilty. He was moved several times during the narration and at the end of it, he promised, of his own will, to work hard and carry these lessons with him all his Life. As a parent, if you had been in my place, isn't that all you would have wanted too?

Vaani and I are often asked what we would have done if Aanchal too wanted to go to the US or anywhere overseas for her under-graduation, just like her brother did. Well, the answer is, we would have sent her. Because we believe the Universe would have taken care of her, just as it took care of Aashirwad. However, the real story is that Aanchal wants to be a dance therapist and is training in dance in Chennai, along with studying for a Psychology degree in a college here and feels she would be better off going to the US, in 2015, for a post-graduate programme in dance and movement therapy. We simply trust her choice.

Give your children strong values and teach them how to fly. As a parent, these are your *only* two responsibilities. Beyond this, they need nothing from you. Teach them what's right and what's wrong but don't force them to agree with you on either. Teach them forgiveness, don't insist they do. Teach them the value of money, but don't demand that they avoid taking risks. Teach them to love, care and be good, don't expect that they immediately will. Basically, don't try to live their lives. Trust them and yourself. They are *your* children, they will be fine. Keep reminding them that the doors to your home and heart are always open for them, so that when they do want to come back to share, to confess, to catch up, to just cuddle up, they are always welcome. Being a responsible parent is a rewarding and important part of intelligent living! Responsible parenting means grooming and leading happy, young adults to take over from you at home!

Don't Judge Anyone If You Have Not Been On Their Path Yourself!

Way back in 1993, while working for *Businessworld* magazine as their Principal Correspondent in Bengaluru, I had written an elaborate story on how Vijay Mallya's business empire was debt-ridden and that he was broke and cash-strapped. (Interestingly, as I write this Afterword, media reports suggest that Mallya's business group's present condition appears to be the same!) I remember waiting in Mallya's UB Group headquarters (where the present day UB

City[130] is located) for 15 hours at a stretch because he was trying to avoid the interview. I even slept on the couch in his private lounge refusing to leave despite his EA's insistence. This was to be *the* interview of my journalistic career and I was not going to give up! Finally, I managed to get Mallya's time and his version of why his businesses were struggling. We ran the story, titling it *'An Acquired Hangover'* and showing a completely sloshed Mallya at his Kunigal[131] stud farm. Our photographer Deepak Pawar (at that time, he was a freelancer) had counted the number of mugs of beer that Mallya had drunk in the three hours we spent interviewing him: 16! He had waited for the very end of the interview to get his shot to 'fit' the story's central theme: that it was a series of reckless acquisitions that had landed Mallya in this mess.

I have nothing to say about Mallya's business decisions then or now, about his cash problems then or now. Not anymore. All I feel is, irrespective of what caused his crisis, or mine, the pain is the same. Every single day through this bankruptcy, and even now, I have regretted the way we led that story asking, critically, sarcastically, logically,

---

[130]UB City – the UB Group, Mallya's business group, headquarters were located here on Vittal Mallya Road, Bengaluru; in 2008, a luxury mall came up in its place.
[131]Kunigal – a small town 75 kms away on the outskirts of Bengaluru where Vijay Mallya owns a stud farm and breeds horses that he races in Indian derbies.

pointedly, argumentatively, "Why is Vijay Mallya at a loss for cash?" I am not even saying the story was good or bad. All I am saying is I now know what it means to be strapped for cash. And I now know what it means when every aspect of your Life is scrutinized, dissected, opined upon and judged – only because you don't have money and you have to repay people that you have borrowed from.

Society expects a bankrupt person to be a certain way. To be shorn of certain visible, physical attributes. Attire, Address, Attitude – society expects you to be impacted on all three dimensions. You are expected to live on the pavement, perhaps. You are expected to wear worn out clothes. You are not expected to be found in movie halls or restaurants or travelling Business Class. You are expected to have no friends. You are expected to be lonely and miserable!

Let me tell you what happens in reality. Businesses go bankrupt. Individuals, especially those in business for generations, rarely do. If it is a second generation business, like Mallya's for instance, the family is secure and their assets are available for leverage and some unknown and unaffected (by the bankruptcy) source of personal income may exist as well. But first generation entrepreneurs, like Vaani and me, do not have that kind of luck in the form of assets or savings or personal wealth or an alternate revenue stream to fall back upon.

Vaani and I have, in the last seven years, gone down to the wire, to just a thousand rupees, like what I describe in the beginning of this book, several times over. So, technically, logically, we should be on the street. But that's not what happened to us.

In each of the 24 months between 2008 and 2009, we miraculously found cash coming our way, to help us buy groceries, pay electricity and phone bills, cover fuel and miscellaneous living expenses and pay salaries to our personal staff. Someone always came forward and helped. By our asking them or on their own. While we survived, we could not still pay the rent for our apartment. We could have vacated it and moved into a smaller apartment. To be sure we decided to move into an apartment in Mylapore[132] for a monthly rent of ₹5000 ($100) but we just couldn't manage the ₹50,000 ($1000), we needed to pay, in advance, as rental deposit. We therefore could not vacate our duplex apartment in Bishop Garden, Chennai. Unfortunately, this caused deep anguish to our landlord, who, to be fair, was very patient with us. He finally had to litigate and when it almost seemed like we would be evicted in a month's time, through a court order, a friend volunteered to give us his apartment in the same neighbourhood without rent!

Now, how do you explain that? What would you do in that situation? With a teenaged daughter and

---

[132]Mylapore – a congested middle-class area in South Chennai.

an 80-year-old father-in-law to look after? Would you question the rationale behind the Universe's benevolence or would you surrender to it?

As a strategy, in 2009, we wound up our office, and painfully let go of our last client service person and our accountant. We had operated in that office for 13 years. 11 out of the 13 years, we had paid our rent on time. Including in the years of early cash-flow issues: 2002~2007. So much so, that when we announced our decision to vacate the office premises, the landlord said we could continue for a couple of years more if we were confident of getting the business back on track, and his backlogged rents too. He said that in his years of financial stress, it was only the rent that we paid on time, which had helped him survive!

However, our strategy was to handle our business and client delivery ourselves. Our new business model could only be delivered by Vaani and me. So, while we let go of everyone in the Firm, and closed our office, we retained our personal staff. A driver, maid, cook, a personal assistant and an EA. Our logic was that with Vaani and me having to travel on client work, and for us to focus on the bankruptcy situation – which included creditor relations, dealing with legal issues and meeting unknown challenges as and when they surfaced – we needed the home department taken care of. Further, as entrepreneurs, we had a responsibility towards our employees. People with education and professional backgrounds could always seek and get employment elsewhere. But the people, and their families, who depended solely on your employment and were intimately connected with your family over years of working together, cannot be left high and dry. So, we chose not to let go of our home team.

But people expect someone bankrupt to have no staff! In a business, if you don't have manpower, how can you deliver a product or service, profit and claw your way back? The paradigm shift we made was to equip ourselves personally, by retaining our personal staff so that we could manage the clients ourselves, ensuring an unmatched service quality to our clients and a better yield through enhanced billings to us!

We also took certain calls so that Aanchal's or our morale was not affected. A simple thing like a floral arrangement, which used to come bi-weekly, from a very creative florist called Bloom (Amethyst[133]) in Chennai, would cost us ₹350 ($7). We had been having this arrangement delivered for over eight years now. We decided not to do away with it although the service cost us a princely ₹700 ($14) each week. Whenever we saw the arrangement in our living room, it reminded Vaani and me that Life is beautiful and we must

---

[133]Amethyst – a very popular boutique and coffee place in Chennai, a sister store of Chamiers' where much of this book's manuscript was written and edited; Amethyst also runs the florist service, Bloom.

learn to trust Life just like these flowers do! The other area we did not cut down on was the way we maintained our clothes. We had to be presentable. We did not buy new clothes for months on end because we couldn't afford to but we always had them laundered and dry-cleaned with premium service providers so when we wore them, they looked good on us. In our business, interacting with CEOs of large companies and leadership teams is the norm. We could not afford to be dressed inappropriately. So, even if we wore worn-out underclothes, our dresses, shoes, shirts, ties and suits looked immaculate. We also have this habit of keeping our living space squeaky clean. All our furniture at home is old and some of it is even broken but the way Vaani arranges them and the way we maintain our home, it doesn't ever show. Besides, the apartments we have got to live in, have been well designed and in premium neighbourhoods. We never sought any of them. People we know trusted us, wanted to help, and simply gave them to us.

So, we defy the societal definition of a bankrupt family. We live in a nice apartment which is courtesy someone's generosity. We drive a car which is a gift to us. Our son studied in a premium, private under-graduate school in the US during the darkest years of our bankruptcy, because Life willed it so. We have personal staff because only Vaani and I can run the business and even if one of us is not there to deliver, client delivery will suffer.

Yet people judge us without being in our shoes or walking our path.

My own mother chided us for paying our personal staff salaries during this time and wondered why we could not use that cash to repay the amount borrowed from her? My brother, who visited the new apartment we had shifted into three years ago, the one which was given rent-free (gratis) by a friend, thought we had purchased a new 42-inch TV. He demanded to know if we had the money to buy a new TV, why wasn't I able to repay my parents? The truth is something he was unwilling to consider: that TV had been with us for several years by then; we had merely moved it to the living room because we didn't have a separate room for TV viewing in this smaller living space!

Cashlessness does not mean that your Life will come to a standstill. This is what we have come to learn also. Cashlessness means your Life will go on, miraculously, if you trust the Universe, defying odds, defying gravity and defying logic. So, I haven't, as a father been able to provide for my daughter, the way Indian fathers are expected to, when she came of a certain age, but I have seen cash come in each time her school or dance class fees had to be paid. I have not been able to get my wife anything for any of our wedding anniversaries for seven years now. But I have found cash come in to service my 'miracle' car each time so that it does not throw a tantrum and affect, critically, the family's mobility. I have not been able to repay any of my creditors, including my parents, but have had cash come in and provide for many an underprivileged child's education when families have approached us.

We have learnt the following three big lessons: 1. A bankruptcy does not mean the bankrupt don't have the right to live and rebuild. 2. Whatever you need, the Universe will always provide it, if you trust it implicitly to do so. 3. Someone else's crisis and need is always bigger than yours!

In a bankruptcy, people also expect the main protagonists to be unhappy, depressed, mournful and sorrowful. To be honest, initially, we too were, but we soon discovered that being unhappy made the situation no better. Money did not flow through the roof because we were unhappy. Which is again something we have learned. *Being happy is not a crime, just as being broke is not!* So, if you come home, you will find us celebrating Life! As a family, we are always happy. Yes, we do, me in particular, lose it some days and at moments when an unknown, unforeseen development rocks you. In a brief while though, my awareness, harnessed through the daily practice of *mouna*, directs me to know that I am losing it. So, I anchor within and rediscover inner peace in that moment!

Our Life in the last seven years, has defied, as you can see, all conventional perceptions of a bankruptcy. So, on all three fronts, Attitude, Attire and Address, we have not conformed to popular perceptions!

This phase has taught us not to judge anyone – including yourself, if you have not walked their path. Let us never pass judgment. The easiest things that roll off people's tongues are loose words that are petty, unjustified, emotional responses to perceptions we hold about other people. We do this all the time. You may have found it somewhat questionable that I chose to share what I feel about my mother and my siblings and their behaviour towards Vaani, me and our bankruptcy. *I stand by reporting what I have felt.* I have tried not to pass judgment or opine. If you or they believe I have been judgmental, I seek your – and their – understanding and forgiveness. Through reporting what I have learned from what I have felt, I have tried to share a way of living intelligently and peacefully.

We must recognize and appreciate that we are all a product of the time we go through. That we are all continuously evolving. Our behaviours are manifestations of what we think. What we think is representative of what we experience. If we experience joy, we are thinking and operating from the core of happiness. Hence we come across as anchored, fun-loving people, easy to get along with. When we experience pain, rejection, criticism, and we don't know how to handle them, we are thinking from a depressive spiral. Our behaviour at such times can vary from being cold to cranky to cantankerous to vindictive! Whenever you see someone behaving like this, or when a child or team member is not performing to their potential, examine not just the symptoms. Go to the cause. The behaviour is symptomatic of a cause which could have its roots, at times, in the state of the person's mental or physical health. People who don't live up to your expectations need your help. They don't need your opinions. There's a tendency for us to look for sweeping generalizations about the behaviour of people around us, without knowing what people are going through. Every beating heart has a story that you and I don't know of. So, let's not judge. Let's not pass judgment. If we can't reach out, or help, or make a difference, let us, at least, not kill with words or our opinions!

Everything, Absolutely Everything, Happens For A Reason!

In the summer of 2013, an irate creditor filed a complaint against me in another Indian state. He must have pulled many strings using his influence, among politicians and the police in his city to be able to present his case as having been 'cheated' by me. His efforts resulted in a FIR (First Information Report) being filed against me under Section 420 of the Indian Penal Code. Now, when a case is booked under that Section, the cops have to first convince themselves that there was a *prima facie* intent to cheat. The cops, in this case, appeared to have overlooked that criteria. Because had they actually considered it carefully they would have been convinced that I had been all along, often proactively, communicating with this creditor – over email, SMS and in person – expressing my inability to repay him immediately. They would then have had to allow this matter to be treated as a civil dispute, which could only be decided upon by a relevant court, and not be treated as a criminal offence like cheating. But my creditor had ensured just the opposite! A cop 'investigating' the matter called me up to tell me that he was coming over to Chennai to pick me up – a move which normally would result in the accused (in this case, me) scrounging up the money somehow to avoid being arrested. But Vaani and I had no cash. So, for us, the cop's call clearly meant I would be arrested and presented in court in the city, in another state, where the FIR had been lodged.

Business has been virtually nil since mid-2012, post Aashirwad's graduation, and we simply had no money. I could seek both anticipatory bail or apply for bail, after being arrested, but all of this required engaging a lawyer in the other city – and that required money. We had had to sell Vaani's *thali*, which was the last remaining material asset with us, around that time to generate cash to meet our daily living expenses – like groceries, cooking gas and telephone bills. Things were really that grave. Vaani and I decided to face this crisis head-on. We felt that given the gravity of the situation, Aashirwad (who had by then moved to Denver, Colorado, from Chicago, to take up a job) and Aanchal, and my parents, had to be informed.

The idea was to just share this update so they didn't feel left out in any way. Particularly, given the acrimony that surrounded us in my family, I didn't want Vaani to face any taunts (*for 'getting' me arrested!*) from my mother!

I called my mother on Friday, June 21, 2013. We were speaking for the first time in over four years. In these years I had learned to forgive her for the way she felt about me. At the same time, I was also quite certain that I may never be able to win her trust again even if I did manage to repay all the money I owed her and the family. The few times we had corresponded on email, in these years, the acrimony had persisted. She continued to say what she always had said and I continued to resist her – with absolutely no success. Each encounter would leave me weaker, saddened and helpless. But my awareness, helped by my daily practice of *mouna,* always came to my rescue. While those debilitating emotions would unfailingly arise within me, my awareness would help me overcome them and remain detached.

But my parents were not getting any younger. And I was growing older too. Somewhere, deep within me, despite my commendable efforts to let go and stay detached, I wondered whether I would ever be able to sit with my parents and tell them that I was not a cheat. That Vaani and I were just caught in a vicious web of circumstance. That, despite all the evidence stacked up against us, we had done nothing unethical. That to be bankrupt was an awakening, a humbling experience. Not a crime. I feared that my parents would die some day and we would never be able to have this conversation. It is bizarre if you can't have an honest conversation with the people that had a role in your creation. That feeling of hopelessness gnawed at me each time I thought about my family and the money I owed them. I actually wanted to talk more to my Dad, whom I related to and who I knew trusted me and Vaani.

That afternoon, on Friday, June 21, 2013, I called my mother. My father has a heart condition. I was not sure I wanted to shock him with the update I had with me of my impending arrest. My mother was surprised and happy I had called. She heard me out.

In a very humble, reassuring manner, she told me, "Nothing will happen to you. Be strong. I will talk to *appa* and call you back." Now, humility is certainly not a trait I associate with my mother. So, I remember wondering why she was sounding different. Maybe four years of estrangement, and no worthwhile communication, can thaw any frozen relationship, I thought.

I simply responded, "I do not want you people alarmed. Vaani and I are very strong. And we will face this. Your son is not a cheat. This call is only to keep you informed lest you turn around and say we kept you in the dark."

My mother surprised me with her answer, "I know you are not a cheat!"

However preposterous I found it to accept her 'revised' opinion of me, I decided not to belabour the point. I had got so used to, and numbed by the pain of being called a cheat by her that it had stopped mattering to me. Besides, an impending arrest, cashlessness, the legal consequences that were to follow if I was arrested – these were issues that were far more critical for me and Vaani to focus on at that time. Certainly more important to me than why, and how, my mother thought of me differently now. In a few more seconds, the call between us had ended. Without pausing to think of that call, I went about spending the rest of the evening preparing, with Vaani, for what lay ahead of us.

The next morning, Saturday, June 22, 2013, my father called me at 7 AM. He invited me to come and meet him and my mother. I had wanted to meet him for several weeks now. So, I immediately agreed. We met at the Café Coffee Day in Indira Nagar, Adayar later that morning.

As we sat down, my mother spoke first. What she said stumped me. *"I am very sorry for all that has happened. I am sorry for all that I have said and done,"* she said, holding my hand. Although I found it hard to believe that she really meant what she said, I was sorry to see her apologize.

I chose to remain unmoved though. I simply told her it was okay. I said I did not want to go into the past. It would not help any of us. More importantly, I feared that my mother and I would be at each other's throats soon – as we had always been in the past – and I didn't want a showdown in a café, of all places! I used that moment to take the opportunity to express myself calmly.

I shared with my parents how Vaani and I feel about being thought of as cheats by most of the family – by my mother, brother and sister. I explained to them what we had been going through (much of the content of this book) and pleaded for their understanding and patience. It was a long meeting. It lasted over four hours. Many times, when I spoke, I broke down – causing other guests in the café and the crew to look in our direction. As long as I spoke, my mother listened. She did not butt in. That, to me, was a miracle – *that my mother paused to listen to me!* Then by turns, my father and my mother spoke. It seemed incredible that this was happening. *We were actually having a conversation, not a fight!*

That evening, when I shared the details of this meeting with Vaani, I told her how grateful I was to this creditor for having precipitated the matter between him and me. Without things coming to a head, like an impending arrest, I wouldn't have called my mother. Without that call, my father would not have called me over the next day. Without that meeting, I would never have been able to tell my parents what I always wanted them to hear from me. The reason behind this present crisis was very purposeful, I told Vaani, one that made the pain, which the crisis had brought in its wake, look inconsequential.

My father is a lawyer (though, at 75, he has retired and appears only for exceptional cases that involve social causes). Having understood the matter relating to this creditor that we were up against, he offered to appear for me in court and also decided to speak with the creditor – both as a father and as a lawyer. I let him do what he thought was right because I was not making much headway with the creditor or in resolving the criminal complaint against me, in any case. So, over the next few days and weeks, my father, along with our legal counsel, S. Vijayaraghavan, crafted a strategy that slowly, but surely, weaned this creditor away from following through with his ruinous plan of 'employing' police action in a purely civil matter. The creditor was eventually convinced that Vaani and I genuinely did not have the means to pay any money now, and was reassured, by my consistent proactive approach and my father's mature conduct, that here was a family that would eventually pay when able. He agreed to work with us to quash, with mutual consent, the FIR that his complaint had caused to be filed against me.

In the time that my father led the strategy to resolve the crisis, I met with my parents several times. At each meeting, I used the opportunity to express myself. I greatly appreciate and respect my mother for listening to me every time I spoke at these meetings. Over these conversations, a sense of dignity and decorum has come to govern my relationship with her. I have helped her to understand that it is perfectly fine for her and for me to have different outlooks to Life. I have told her that while I can never believe she trusts me completely, I am not going to let that feeling ever dictate how I treat her going forward. I have reiterated to her that I will forever be grateful to her for giving birth to me, for raising me and for all that she has taught me and for all that I have learned from her.

I always knew this but now I am convinced beyond doubt – that everything happens for a reason. That reason may not be immediately apparent to us, but sometimes, when you think about the events that have shaped your Life; you may well find that each event had a reason. Honestly, I still don't know what led my mother to call me a cheat; it doesn't matter anymore – because my grief over being called so has long evaporated. But I do know that without that creditor's machinations, I would not be celebrating just how miraculously Life engineered a set of events that have led me to at least have calm, polite conversations with my mother – even if we still can't relate to each other.

Laugh Your Life Away!

Postpone everything else, but don't ever postpone being happy. Because then you will be postponing living itself! Think about it. Despite the situations that we find ourselves in, we still have the choice to smile, laugh and move on. Nobody can take that choice away from us. But we don't quite exercise that choice because we find it convenient to sulk, to brood, to pity ourselves and to lament about what we don't have. Pity is a seductive impersonator. It arrives oozing warmth and comfort. And poor you – and me – fall for its guile. And then pity unleashes its fangs, keeping you in its vice-like grip, pushing you into depression! There is a way out though – make a choice to laugh at your situation, any situation. Laugh! Laugh at yourself. Laugh at the world. Just laugh!

At the end of 2008, Vaani, Aanchal and I went to watch a movie called *Dostana*[134] at the INOX multiplex in Chennai. During the intermission, the person sitting next to me shrieked at seeing me. It was Diwakar Jaisinghania,[135] a financier who had loaned us money. He had been very sympathetic to our situation and saw me and Vaani as being genuine folks. But he could not hide his shock at seeing me that evening.

"*Sirji,*[136] you here?" he asked.

'Why? Shouldn't I be here?" I asked.

"But you don't have money?" he suggested.

---

[134]*Dostana* – meaning Friendship, directed by Tarun Mansukhani.

[135] Real name not disclosed to protect identity.

[136] *Sirji* – colloquial usage for 'Sir' in Hindi.

"I don't have money to pay you but I do have money to buy movie tickets for the three of us," I explained.

"But I also mean that you have so many problems, how can you be happy?" he protested.

I responded with a borrowed line that I use in all my workshops: *"Success is getting what you want. Happiness is wanting what you get!"*

He was awakened, educated and convinced! He thanked me profusely for that insight.

That's really how we have learnt to deal with Life! When you can't make sense of it, you laugh at it! Try this now. Think of your most vexing problem and laugh to yourself. And watch your perspective change. Zoom out and look at what you are faced with in the context of your entire Life. You will find that all that you are going through, just as all that you have gone through in your Life so far, is inconsequential. What is of consequence is that you are alive and can still laugh!

There is no reason I can find to explain all that we have faced and are facing. I can't explain why Vaani and I, having gone bankrupt, should have survived, why this book has been published and why you are reading this now. Yet all of this has happened and none of this is a mistake. Because, the Master Plan, the cosmic design, has no flaws. Everything is perfect in its own place, just the way it should be. It is always what it is. No amount of arguing with Life can change it. Only calm, determined action can change a situation. Over years of practicing patience, we have learnt that it is a continuous, never-ending process.

We have reached a state, which you too can reach; the state the Buddha described thus: "When you realize how perfect things are in your Life, you will look up and laugh at the sky."

Trust Life!

If you think you have not evolved enough yet to be able to laugh away your troubles, then simply learn to *trust* Life! Know that if you have been created, you will also be given the ways and means to last this lifetime. Trusting Life essentially means trusting yourself. No situation has ever been placed before you that you cannot handle. But we don't see Life this way. The problem arises because we don't want to trust Life and instead expect Life to be our hand maiden, doing what we want, which in reality is not the way it works. Look at people in your own Life. Don't you trust some people more than others? And don't you reward people that you trust with more of your time, sharing your innermost feelings, at times even giving them your material assets like money, property, your car and gifts? Would you give any of these to people you don't trust? So, it is with Life. If you trust Life, it will reward you. Just as it has rewarded us by keeping us alive, abundant and awakened!

The Buddha has taught us, "Pain in Life is inevitable. But suffering is optional." So simple, so profound. So, stop fighting Life. Trusting Life means to believe that any situation you are put in is for your own benefit, for you to learn and for you to grow stronger and wiser from the experience.

Trusting Life means to know that we all will have 83 kinds of problems in our Life all the time and if we handle the 84th problem, we will not have any of the first 83! Perplexed? Let me share a Zen story I have heard:

Once upon a time, long ago, there was a village at the foot of a mountain. On top of the mountain there lived a wise old lady. She sat around a fire all day and drank herbal tea. Whenever the villagers had a problem and needed wisdom, they would go to her (although it was quite a climb to the top of the mountain). One day there was this guy, who had a problem and needed wisdom, so he put on his climbing gear and reached the summit of the mountain.

When he reached the top, the old lady saw him and shouted: "I know why you are here!"

He shouted back: "You do? Why?"

She answered: "Because you have a problem."

The bloke thought to himself, "Big deal. Anyone could have guessed that!" But he walked closer anyway.

When he got there, she told him, "I know you have a problem because everyone has problems – 83 to be exact. Yes, everybody has 83 problems."

The guy looked a bit baffled and asked the woman how she had worked that one out. She replied, "Everyone has 83 problems and your job is to solve them. But be assured that when you wake up tomorrow morning, you will have 83 problems again. It's a constant. In other words, if you solve 50 of your 83 problems today, they will be topped up back to 83 tomorrow."

"That's quite depressing," the guy answered.

"Aah, but that's the biggest problem of them all. Actually it's the 84th problem," said the old lady, continuing, "It's the biggest one and actually the only one, because if you solve that one, you erase the effects of the other 83!"

The guy thought to himself that this woman couldn't have been great at math when she was in school, but he replied anyway, "And what is this 84th problem?"

The old lady gave him a wicked smile and said, "Thinking that you shouldn't have problems. That's the 84th problem. You see, most people think that they shouldn't have any problems and when they wake up every morning and find their 83 problems; they become depressed, because they think they shouldn't have them at all. Now they start solving them with the hope that when they are solved, they will be gone forever and they can focus on other things. So while they struggle to solve these problems they forget about the positives in their Life. They reckon they can focus on living when

– and after – they have solved their problems. So they put their family, children, dogs, hobbies and sadly even their dreams on hold, so they can get this source of irritation out of the way. Then, they wake up the next morning with their 83 problems topped up again."

"So what should I do?" the man asked.

"When you accept that you will always have problems, they will shrink in significance and although the issues will still be there, you will view them as opportunities to grow and learn. Go forth, my son. Embrace your problems and be thankful, for they are opportunities to make you a better person," advised the wise old lady.

Hear her out. She's Lady Life. Speaking to *you*. Trust Life and therefore trust yourself. It makes perfect strategic sense because there's no other way to live and besides, the rewards accrue only when you trust yourself – implicitly.

Have Integrity Of Purpose, All Else Will Follow!

Many a time, I have been asked if by being accepting of our situation, haven't we resigned to fate, given up, turned defeatist? I want to tell you what I always tell people. While being accepting, we visualize every rupee being paid back, to every single creditor, with the full interest due on each borrowing. While being accepting, we have been available, accessible and responsive to every single creditor. We are often chided for being cashless but none, barring my own family, has told us that we are dishonest. We have learned to: 1. Just be. 2. While just being, be at it. You too may like to learn this.

Arriving at this state of awareness does not take time or practice, it only takes a moment of awakening. When you let Life take you on its course, you just be, you don't resist, you don't fight, you don't agonize and so you are peaceful and often in bliss. But letting Life flow on its own terms does not mean stopping what you must do. This is the action that the *Gita*[137] talks about. This is the duty; this is the Purpose that creation has intended for us. When you are not aware or 'awake', you try multiple things, you try to control, you fight and you worry. When the awakening moment happens, when your Purpose finds you, you find meaning in doing what you must do. In getting to that moment of awakening is where most of mankind fails to employ the intellect it is endowed with. We see this intellect demonstrated ever so often: in a smart business deal, in an invention, in the way we convince an airline agent to confirm a waitlisted booking, in arguing a point, in making important investment decisions. Yet, in the most critical aspect of our journey through this planet, we miss the opportunity to employ our

---

[137] *Gita* – The Bhagavad Gita, the holy Hindu text, considered a very relevant manual for 'intelligent living'.

intellect. That awakening moment could be right now, if we accepted in all humility that there must be a reason for our creation (*raison d'être*) and if we seek for Life to unveil it to us.

Life has revealed our Purpose to Vaani and me – which is, to awaken people to the right way of thinking, living, working and winning. This Purpose inspires our every waking moment. Taking crucial decisions, over which the mind can dither and agonize endlessly, have become simple for us. Be it pledging our gold jewellery to raise cash or sending Aashirwad to Chicago or letting an irate creditor do whatever he deems right or confronting a client, who has money but is not ethical, or confessing to a parent that our chemistry doesn't work! Our doggedness to stay on the path and last the journey stems from knowing our Purpose. We know all else will follow!

Namaste!

The ancient Indian tradition of greeting one another with folded hands is called *'namaste'*. It actually means that the God within you bows to the God within another when you wish that person *'namaste'*!

Through this experience, I have learned that in Life, there is no external God. Each of us has the godhead in us. It is the energy that powers us; it is divine and is what causes all our miracles. The miracles I have shared with you have been caused because Vaani and I see Life, and its every moment, as a continuous miracle.

Even our debt is a miracle! We don't know where our lives will take us in the future. We have not even started earning enough to begin repaying our debt. But we know that the Life that brought us to debt will also get us out of it! We have learned to love our debt because without this debt, we wouldn't have seen God in each person who has crossed our path. Without this debt we wouldn't have learned the art of living in this world and yet being above it! Without this debt we wouldn't have been able to teach our children the true meaning of Life!

When Aashirwad graduated from the University of Chicago on Saturday, June 9, 2012, Vaani and I gave him a unique graduation hat. It was a wall-mountable portrait of a graduation hat made by a freelance artist and graphic designer in Bengaluru, whom we have not even met, called Sowmya Nagarajan. This graduation hat is not filled with colour. It has the names of all the 179 Angels – our creditors, including friends and family, to whom we owe money – who have come forward and helped reiterate our faith in humanity – in maroon (the University of Chicago colour) text on a white background. We gave it to Aashirwad so that he remembers, when hubris strikes him, just as it does strike everyone, that he owes his education and career to these 179 people. To us, as a family, that constellation of 179 people is divine and each of them is God. We bow to them in worship daily.

Let me conclude by telling you another story of my Life. In the summer of 2010, I was afflicted with a chronic episode of Rheumatoid Arthritis (RA). In my case, this auto-immune disease affects my upper back. Standing, sitting, walking, even turning on my side in bed, became a nightmare. For 45 days, I could not even stand up. In those days, an understanding client in Pune paid us a retainer even though I could not physically travel to work with their team. I conducted my meetings with them on Skype and over phone in the days that I was immobile. Thanks to this client we survived that phase. At the end of May 2010, another client called us for a full-day workshop to Chittoor.[138] Vaani requested the client to send us a good car because of my back condition and also forewarned the client that I may not be able deliver the full workshop on my feet. The client had worked with us in the past and was considerate enough to allow me to sit down and conduct the workshop. In great pain, thanks to the poor condition of the roads, I arrived in Chittoor with Vaani on Tuesday, June 1, 2010. I woke up with acute pain at 3 AM the next morning. I struggled through preparing for the workshop and my bath. At 9.30 AM, I took 30 minutes to walk to the banquet hall of the hotel where we were staying, a distance of hardly a hundred feet from our room, where my session was to be held!

---

[138]Chittoor – a district headquarter in Andhra Pradesh, a South Indian state.

80 managers and senior executives awaited me in the banquet hall. After our client's Human Resources Head introduced me, I rose with much difficulty and in great pain to conduct my workshop. I am a high-energy workshop leader who likes to pump up the audience, provoke their thinking and bring them alive! Despite writhing in pain, I was sure I had to do it again that day. I started cautiously but as the day wore on, I just let go. Barring a 30-minute lunch break, I stood all through the eight hours leading and delivering one of the most transformational, personally for me too, workshops I have ever conducted. To be sure, I healed during those eight hours and have not had another debilitating episode of RA in over 40 months so far! What happened of my RA? Of my 45-day back problem? How did I stand and deliver a workshop, moving, jumping, singing, dancing and energizing my audience, for eight hours?

The answers to all questions lie in my letting go. I just let the Universe and Life take over. Only when we let go and move on will we see newer horizons. When you let go, you are free, unfettered and are ready to go where you want to and where nobody ever has gone before! Our true work is living, and travelling the journey of Life, moving on and on!

All of us like to believe that we are in control of our lives. That we make our own destinies. We become self-centred and begin to see everything only from one point of view. But Life doesn't work like that. It has a mind of its own. Always remember, you are made to go through each experience for a reason. When things don't go your way, you get angry and frustrated. In some time, after much kicking around, you will realize that fighting and resisting Life is futile. Instead, isn't it far simpler to just let go? And take each day as it comes, accepting Life for what it is?

Dear reader, I am not sure if this book has changed the way you look at your Life. It would be great, if it has. Even so, I will always be happy for the opportunity it has given me to share. And for helping you remember, most certainly, that when Life overtakes you, as it often will, let Life take over. And you, you simply trust Life and ***fall like a rose petal!***

Namaste!
AVIS Viswanathan
Chennai
November 2013

The Universal Prayer

Through this experience, I have lost all interest in religion, as it is preached and practised today. I find it ritualistic and divisive. In the name of pluralism it alienates us from each other. They say spirituality is the flowering of inner awareness. They also say religion is for those who want to go to heaven, and spirituality is for those who have been to hell! I have been to hell and I identify with both these sayings closely.

I composed this prayer on my mobile phone on Sunday, December 23, 2007. It was a fervent plea from me to Life to show me the right way, through the labyrinth of fear, anxiety and uncertainty that tormented me at that time. It has since become a prayer to Life, whom I have come to recognize as the only God and the greatest Teacher. To me, Life is the Higher Energy that embraces and nurtures all creation. That's why all through this book Life is spelt with a capital 'L'! Each day, during my *mouna* session, I pray to Life, reciting this prayer slowly, savouring each word, and relating it to my experiences of the previous day. Since I don't understand Sanskrit, and since most Indian Hindu prayers are composed in that language, I have been unable to relate to any of them seriously. English, however, as a medium, helps me internalize each sentiment and embed daily learnings firmly in my soul!

You too can try it. Peace and joy are both intended and assured outcomes!

Teach me O Teacher...

Each day as I arise and awake, teach me to be humble. Teach me to respect another Life and to accept that just as I am entitled to my opinion, others are too. Teach me to contribute selflessly and without expectation.

Teach me O Teacher, to forgive every act of unkindness and injustice. Teach me to unlearn and forget what may not be relevant to me as I journey along.

Teach me O Teacher, to conquer anger and to attain that state of *ahimsa*,[139] when all violence inside me subsides, and true love prevails. Teach me to overcome hatred and jealousy.

Teach me to avoid ruinous temptations and to employ discretion at such times that I may waver.

Teach me O Teacher, to soak in the silence that engulfs me and for me to discover the real me in it. Teach me to lead a Life of action, skilfully and selflessly, to live in this world and yet be above it.

Teach me O Teacher, to remain detached from the fruits of my actions and to know that if the motive is pure and the means are correct, in the end it will all be fine if I do my best and leave you the rest.

Teach me O Teacher, to be eternally grateful for this Life and this experience!

---

[139]'*Ahimsa*' – a Sanskrit word meaning a state of non-violent thought and action.

Most Grateful

"If the only prayer you ever say in your whole Life is 'thank you', that would suffice."

~ Meister Eckhart,
German Philosopher and Mystic (1260~1327)

I am eternally grateful to all these people who have touched and shaped my Life and have made this book possible:

My mother, Geetha – for giving birth to me, raising me and teaching me the alphabet.

Shirdi Baba – you taught me Faith and Patience. Without your influence on my Life I would not have lasted this time.

Swami Sathya Sai Baba – *our* Swami. How can I even describe what you have done and continue to do for us? I know you are with me, with us, every step of the way. This book would not have been possible without your energy, presence, essence and grace.

Vaani, *Mom* – for all your love and for walking alongside me! For bearing with me, for critiquing this effort, for making it happen!

Aash and Aanch – for giving us joy, every single day, for being mature, responsible, caring and compassionate, for giving me the medium to express myself so that you, and now others too, can learn.

Deepak Pawar – my *Guru*, for unmasking me and showing me the road to living intelligently!

Gautam Padmanabhan, Paul Vinay Kumar and Karthik Venkatesh at Westland – for seeing value in sharing our experiences and learnings with the world! Radhika Mukherjee, my editor, who has embellished this work, while helping preserve the soul and message of my story!

Prakash Idnani – for helping Vaani and me envision on a 70 MM canvas!

Jai Subramaniam – for guiding me on my way to being published.

P. C. Bala – for helping me understand what publishers expect from authors.

Snehal Kulshreshtha – for being prophetic in October 2007, when I had called you to share our plight. You told me, "Write a book AVIS! Tell your story! Share so that the world can learn from your experience."

Sudhir 'Obs' Narasimhan – for always reminding me that this book will *have* to be written.

Dr. Daniel Gottlieb – whose '*Letters to Sam*' touched my soul when I first read it and invoked in me the desire to chronicle our experience and bequeath our learnings for our children, for posterity.

Each of my 50 classmates from the PSBB KKN (Chennai) 1984 batch and to our Yahoo Group – where I share a daily learning as 'Thought for the Day'. Without their tolerating my overbearing prolificity, I may never have got down to capturing this experience as a book!

Kiran Rao and Mathangi Srinivasamurti – whose warm smiles, and their Chamiers Café's calm and peace, invited me, almost weekly, between September 2012 and November 2013. It is at this café that this book's manuscript was written, edited, cleaned up and dispatched to Westland. Calvin, Thang, Vishnuvardhan, Ali, Jeffrey, Sebastian and the entire crew at the café, thanks for all the green tea and soups that nourished me through this time.

Amitabh Bachchan – my idol and inspiration. My heart goes out in gratitude to you. You, in an interview to Vir Sanghvi on *Star World*, aired sometime in 2000, shared with the world what it means to have lived through a bankruptcy. Vaani and I have watched that interview every time we have felt depressed, and that has been many, many, many times, in the last seven years.

Osho – whose teachings have simplified Life for me in more ways than I can even describe.

Eknath Easwaran – who introduced me to *Gandhi: The Man*. That's a book that taught me the power of, and in, spirituality!

S. Vijayaraghavan – who pulled out all the stops, and crafted the most ethical strategy one could manage in our circumstances, to protect us on the legal front. We owe a lot to your juniors too – Vivek, Jaishree, Ramesh, Jayaraman, Jaishankar, Anandhi, Dharma Kumar and the late Ramdas. You also constantly encouraged us to keep the faith. It was due to your continuous endeavour that we did not lose our morale! Without you, and your charming wife Ramya's gracious hospitality whenever we called on you, we may well have lost our way!

Harpal Singh – who apart from being a true friend and spending hours on the phone in the early months of the bankruptcy, just allowing me to share, also connected us to an angel, our legal counsel in NCR,[140] Ajay Sharma, whom we are yet to meet! Ajay thanks for believing in our story and standing up for us!

Balan Nair and Ramamohan Nair – the world's finest astrologers, for guiding us and keeping us charged and on the path.

Murugesan and Kannusamy – our dear friends, whose spiritual inspirations have helped us survive those days, months and years, when there wasn't even a ray of hope!

Kavi Rajan – for teaching us to embrace our debt, to love it and to learn from it, rather than run away from it!

---

[140] NCR – refers to the National Capital Region around New Delhi.

Kannan – *my motivator*, for always believing in me, even when I didn't believe in myself!

Venks Venkatachalam – Vaani's father, my spiritual friend, who lives with us and has lived through this traumatic phase without protest, interference or opinion; always blessing us with his wit and equanimity.

Sowmya Nagarajan – the young artist and graphic designer whom we still haven't met in person, but who has designed this book's cover so brilliantly – and so graciously!

Sobha Ravi – my Executive Assistant, for your patience, diligence and unquestioning spirit of support – without which managing these years may have been so much more arduous and this book, well nigh impossible to write!

Francis – my Personal Assistant, for your loyalty and indefatigable on-the-road spirit. Despite driving me up the wall on more than at least a million occasions, you ensured I didn't have to pound the pavement for chores that I simply loathed!

Kumar Narayanan – my young friend, for his boundless energy and for teaching me to trust Life!

My dear father, A. Kasi Viswanathan – who despite all the provocation, and perhaps with evidence pointing to the contrary, chose to trust me and Vaani. I am sorry *Dad* for all that has happened. I want to assure you that we will overcome and emerge 'winners', the way you have always believed we will!

Finally, Life – for the gift of this lifetime, for the miracle of this bankruptcy and for the treasure of this experience! Without providence, I wouldn't have encountered this Life-changing crisis, and therefore, would never have found my true Self, and would have also never known what it is to trust Life and ***fall like a rose petal***!